Hugo's Sim

# French
# Phrase Book

Hugo's Language Books Limited

This edition
© 1986 Hugo's Language Books Ltd/Lexus Ltd
All rights reserved
ISBN 0 85285 082 4


Compiled by
Lexus Ltd
with
Valérie Dupin
and
Karen McAulay

*Facts and figures given in this book were
correct when printed. If you discover any
changes, please write to us.*

8th impression 1992

Set in 9/9 Plantin Light by
Typesetters Ltd and
Printed and Bound by
Courier International Limited
East Kilbride

# CONTENTS

# PREFACE

This is the latest in a long line of Hugo Phrase Books and is of excellent pedigree, having been compiled by experts to meet the general needs of tourists and business travellers. Arranged under the usual headings of 'Hotels', 'Motoring' and so forth, the ample selection of useful words and phrases is supported by an 1800-line mini-dictionary. By cross-reference to this, scores of additional phrases may be formed. There is also an extensive menu guide listing approximately 600 dishes or methods of cooking and presentation.

The pronunciation of words and phrases in the main text is imitated in English sound syllables, and highlighted sections illustrate some of the replies you may be given and the signs or instructions you may see or hear.

# PRONUNCIATION

When reading the imitated pronunciation, the same value should be given to all syllables as there is practically no stress in French words. Pronounce each syllable as if it formed part of an English word, and you will be understood sufficiently well. Remember the points below, and your pronunciation will be even closer to the correct French. Use our audio cassette of selected extracts from this book, and you should be word-perfect!

*ON* represents the nasal sound of 'o'

*AN* represents the nasal sound of 'a'

*OO* is how we imitate the French 'u' (say 'seen' with your lips rounded as if you were about to whistle, and the result will be close enough).

# USEFUL EVERYDAY PHRASES

**Yes/No**
Oui/Non
*wee/nON*

**Thank you**
Merci
*mairsee*

**No thank you**
Non, merci
*nON mairsee*

**Please**
S'il vous plaît
*seel voo pleh*

**I don't understand**
Je ne comprends pas
*juh nuh comprON pa*

**Do you speak English/German/Spanish?**
Parlez-vous anglais/allemand/espagnol?
*parlay voo ONgleh/allmON/espan-yol*

**I can't speak French**
Je ne parle pas français
*juh nuh parl pa frON-seh*

**Please speak more slowly**
Pouvez-vous parler plus lentement, s'il vous plaît?
*poovay voo parlay plOO lentmON, seel voo pleh*

**Please write it down for me**
Pouvez-vous l'écrire, s'il vous plaît?
*poovay voo laykreer, seel voo pleh*

**Good morning/good afternoon/good night**
Bonjour/bonjour/bonsoir
*bONjoor/bONjoor/bONsswahr*

**Goodbye**
Au revoir
*oh-rvwahr*

**How are you?**
Comment allez-vous?
*kommONt allay voo*

**Excuse me please**
Pardon
*pardON*

**Sorry!**
Pardon!
*pardON*

**I'm really sorry**
Je suis vraiment désolé(e)
*juh swee vrayhmON dayzolay*

**Can you help me?**
Pouvez-vous m'aider?
*poovay voo mehday*

**Can you tell me...?**
Pouvez-vous me dire...?
*poovay voo muh deer*

**Can I have ...?**
J'aimerais...
*jemmereh*

**I would like ...**
Je voudrais ...
*juh voodreh*

**Can I pay by cheque?**
Est-ce que je peux payer par chèque?
*esskuh juh puh payay par shek*

**Do you take credit cards?**
Acceptez-vous les cartes de crédit?
*akkseptay voo lay kart duh kraydee*

**Is there ... here?**
Y a-t-il ... ici?
*ee-ateel ... ee-see*

**Where can I get...?**
Savez-vous où je peux trouver...?
*sahvay voo oo juh puh troovay*

**Where is the lavatory please?**
Où sont les toilettes, s'il vous plaît?
*oo sON lay twallet seel voo pleh*

**How much is it?**
Combien ça coûte?
*kombyAN sah koot*

**What time is it?**
Quelle heure est-il?
*kell er eteel*

## USEFUL EVERYDAY PHRASES

**I must go now**
Il faut que je parte
*eel foh kuh juh part*

**Cheers!**
Santé!
*sONtay*

**Go away!**
Allez-vous en!
*allay vooz ON*

## *THINGS YOU'LL SEE OR HEAR*

| | |
|---|---|
| **Arrivée(s)** | arrival(s) |
| **Ascenceur** | lift, elevator |
| **Au revoir** | goodbye |
| **Avancez** | go forward |
| **Bonjour** | hello |
| **Bureau d'accueil** | information desk |
| **Caisse** | till, cash point |
| **Circulez** | move on |
| **Complet** | no vacancies |
| **Départ(s)** | departure(s) |
| **Douane** | customs |
| **Droite** | right |
| **Emplacement réservé** | no parking |
| **En dérangement** | out of order |
| **En panne** | out of order |
| **Entrée** | entrance |
| **Entrée gratuite** | admission free |
| **Entrée interdite** | no entry |
| **Entrée libre** | admission free |
| **Entrez** | come in |
| **Entrez sans frapper** | come straight in |
| **Fermé** | closed |
| **Fermeture annuelle** | annual closure |
| **Fermeture automatique des portes** | doors close automatically |
| **Frappez avant d'entrer** | knock before entering |
| **Fumeurs** | smoking |
| **Gare** | station |
| **Gauche** | left |
| **Heures d'ouverture** | opening hours |
| **Hôpital** | hospital |
| **Horaire** | timetable |

$\longrightarrow$

| | |
|---|---|
| **Il est interdit de marcher sur les pelouses** | keep off the grass |
| **Interdiction de fumer** | no smoking |
| **Libre** | free |
| **Merci** | thank you |
| **Ne pas ... sous peine d'amende** | ... will be fined |
| **Non fumeurs** | no smoking |
| **Non merci** | no thanks |
| **Nous n'acceptons pas les chèques** | cheques not accepted |
| **Objets trouvés** | lost property office |
| **Occupé** | engaged |
| **Ouvert** | open |
| **Papiers, s'il vous plaît** | identity papers, please |
| **Pardon!** | sorry! |
| **Passage interdit** | no entry |
| **Payer à l'ordre de ...** | payable to ... |
| **Payez ici** | pay here |
| **Poussez** | push |
| **Prenez un ticket** | take a ticket |
| **Privé** | private |
| **Reculez** | move back |
| **Renseignements** | enquiries |
| **Réservé** | reserved |
| **Roulez au pas** | drive at walking pace |
| **Rue piétonne** | pedestrian precinct |
| **Rue piétonnière** | pedestrian precinct |
| **Sans issue** | dead end |
| **Sortie** | exit |
| **Tirez** | pull |
| **Toilettes** | gents, ladies |
| **Tout droit** | straight on |

# DAYS, MONTHS, SEASONS

| | | |
|---|---|---|
| **Sunday** | dimanche | *deemONsh* |
| **Monday** | lundi | *lANdee* |
| **Tuesday** | mardi | *mardee* |
| **Wednesday** | mercredi | *merkredee* |
| **Thursday** | jeudi | *juhdee* |
| **Friday** | vendredi | *vONdredee* |
| **Saturday** | samedi | *sammdee* |
| | | |
| **January** | janvier | *jONvee-ay* |
| **February** | février | *fayvree-ay* |
| **March** | mars | *mars* |
| **April** | avril | *ahvreel* |
| **May** | mai | *meh* |
| **June** | juin | *jwAN* |
| **July** | juillet | *jOO-ee-ay* |
| **August** | août | *oo* |
| **September** | septembre | *septombr* |
| **October** | octobre | *octobr* |
| **November** | novembre | *novombr* |
| **December** | décembre | *dayssombr* |
| | | |
| **Spring** | le printemps | *prANtON* |
| **Summer** | l'été | *laytay* |
| **Autumn** | l'automne | *lotton* |
| **Winter** | l'hiver | *leevair* |
| | | |
| **Christmas** | Noël | *no-elle* |
| **Christmas Eve** | le réveillon de Noël | *rayvay-yON duh no-elle* |
| **Good Friday** | Vendredi saint | *vONdredee sAN* |
| **Easter** | Pâques | *pak* |
| **New Year** | le jour de l'an | *joor duh lON* |
| **New Year's Eve** | le réveillon du jour de l'an | *rayvay-yON dOO joor duh lON* |
| **Whitsun** | la Pentecôte | *pontkoht* |

# NUMBERS

| | | |
|---:|---|---|
| 0 | zéro | *zayro* |
| 1 | un, une | *AN, OOn* |
| 2 | deux | *duh* |
| 3 | trois | *trwah* |
| 4 | quatre | *kattr* |
| 5 | cinq | *sANk* |
| 6 | six | *seess* |
| 7 | sept | *set* |
| 8 | huit | *weet* |
| 9 | neuf | *nuhf* |
| 10 | dix | *deess* |
| 11 | onze | *ONz* |
| 12 | douze | *dooz* |
| 13 | treize | *trez* |
| 14 | quatorze | *kattorz* |
| 15 | quinze | *kANz* |
| 16 | seize | *sez* |
| 17 | dix-sept | *dees-set* |
| 18 | dix-huit | *dees-weet* |
| 19 | dix-neuf | *dees-nuhf* |
| 20 | vingt | *vAN* |
| 21 | vingt et un | *vANtay AN* |
| 22 | vingt-deux | *vANt duh* |
| 30 | trente | *trONt* |
| 40 | quarante | *karrONt* |
| 50 | cinquante | *sANkONt* |
| 60 | soixante | *swassONt* |
| 70 | soixante-dix | *swassONt-deess* |
| 80 | quatre-vingts | *kattruhvAN* |
| 90 | quatre-vingt-dix | *kattruh-vANdeess* |
| 100 | cent | *sON* |
| 110 | cent-dix | *sONdeess* |
| 200 | deux cents | *duh-sON* |
| 1000 | mille | *meel* |
| 1,000,000 | un million | *meelliON* |

# TIME

| | | |
|---|---|---|
| **today** | aujourd'hui | *ohjoord-wee* |
| **yesterday** | hier | *yair* |
| **tomorrow** | demain | *duhmAN* |
| **the day before yesterday** | avant-hier | *avONt-yair* |
| **the day after tomorrow** | après-demain | *apreh-duhmAN* |
| **this week** | cette semaine | *set suhmen* |
| **last week** | la semaine dernière | *suhmen dairnee-air* |
| **next week** | la semaine prochaine | *suhmen proshen* |
| **this morning** | ce matin | *suh mattAN* |
| **this afternoon** | cet après-midi | *set apreh-meedee* |
| **this evening** | ce soir | *suh swahr* |
| **tonight** | ce soir | *suh swahr* |
| **yesterday afternoon** | hier après-midi | *yair apreh-meedee* |
| **last night** | hier soir | *yair swahr* |
| **tomorrow morning** | demain matin | *duhmAN mattAN* |
| **tomorrow night** | demain soir | *duhmAN swahr* |
| **in three days** | dans trois jours | *dON trwah joor* |
| **three days ago** | il y a trois jours | *eelee-ya trwah joor* |
| **late** | tard | *tar* |
| **early** | tôt | *toh* |
| **soon** | bientôt | *byANtoh* |
| **later on** | plus tard | *plOO tar* |
| **at the moment** | maintenant | *mANtnON* |
| **second** | seconde | *suhgONd* |
| **minute** | minute | *meenOOt* |
| **ten minutes** | dix minutes | *dee meenOOt* |
| **quarter of an hour** | un quart d'heure | *kar der* |
| **half an hour** | une demi-heure | *duhmee er* |
| **three quarters of an hour** | trois quarts d'heure | *trwah kar der* |
| **hour** | une heure | *er* |
| **day** | un jour | *joor* |

| **week** | une semaine | *suhmen* |
|---|---|---|
| **fortnight, 2 weeks** | quinze jours | *kANz joor* |
| **month** | un mois | *mwah* |
| **year** | une année (un an) | *annay (ON)* |

## TELLING THE TIME

The 24-hour clock is always used both in the written form, as in timetables, and verbally in enquiry offices. However, in everyday life people will use the 12-hour clock.

| **one o'clock** | une heure | *OOn er* |
|---|---|---|
| **ten past one** | une heure dix | *OOn er deess* |
| **quarter past one** | une heure et quart | *OOn er ay kar* |
| **twenty past two** | deux heures vingt | *duhzer vAN* |
| **half past one** | une heure et demie | *OOn er ay duhmee* |
| **twenty to two** | deux heures moins vingt | *duhzer mwAN vAN* |
| **quarter to two** | deux heures moins le quart | *duhzer mwAN luh kar* |
| **ten to two** | deux heures moins dix | *duhzer mwAN deess* |
| **two o'clock** | deux heures | *duhzer* |
| **13.00 (1 pm)** | treize heures | *trez er* |
| **16.30 (4.30 pm)** | seize heures trente | *sez er trONt* |
| **20.10 (8.10 pm)** | vingt heures dix | *vANter deess* |
| **at half past five** | à cinq heures et demie | *ah sANk er ay duhmee* |
| **at seven o'clock** | à sept heures | *ah set er* |
| **noon** | midi | *meedee* |
| **midnight** | minuit | *meenwee* |

# HOTELS

France has over 17,000 hotels officially classified as Tourist Hotels by the Ministère du Commerce. These are identified by a blue and white hexagonal-shaped sign which shows the exact category of the hotel. These categories are: one star HRT: plain but fairly comfortable hotel; two stars HT: good average hotel; three stars HGTGC: very comfortable; four stars HTGC: top class hotel; four stars L: luxury hotel. More information can be obtained from: Direction du Tourisme, 17 rue de l'Ingénieur Robert Keller, 75740 Paris Cedex 15.

In addition to the officially classified Tourist Hotels there are many others in which the rates, services and amenities differ considerably. Among these are:

*Relais de Tourisme:* hotel with a limited number of rooms but offering food of a very good standard.

*Relais Routiers:* hotels, but mainly restaurants, situated on main roads. The food is excellent, the accommodation very reasonable and the prices suprisingly low.

*Châteaux-Hôtels et Vieilles Demeures:* usually of a very high standard and situated in beautiful and historical surroundings, they provide first rate food.

*Relais de Campagne:* these are close to the main highways; most of them are in picturesque settings and all provide excellent food.

*Logis et Auberges de France:* this independent chain of hotels situated off the beaten track gives the motorist a rare opportunity to explore the deep countryside. They have to comply with a rigid set of standards as regards food, service and sanitation in order to get financial assistance from the State. The rates are very reasonable.

## USEFUL WORDS AND PHRASES

| | | |
|---|---|---|
| **balcony** | un balcon | *balkON* |
| **bathroom** | la salle de bain | *sal duh bAN* |
| **bed** | le lit | *lee* |
| **bedroom** | la chambre | *shombr* |
| **bill** | la note | *not* |

| | | |
|---|---|---|
| **breakfast** | le petit déjeuner | *puhtee day-juhnay* |
| **dining room** | la salle à manger | *sal ah mONjay* |
| **dinner** | le dîner | *deenay* |
| **double room** | une chambre pour deux personnes | *shombr poor duh pairson* |
| **foyer** | le hall de réception | *ohll duh rayssep-siON* |
| **full board** | la pension complète | *pONssiON komplet* |
| **half board** | la demi-pension | *duhmee pONssiON* |
| **hotel** | un hôtel | *oh-tell* |
| **key** | la clé/clef | *klay* |
| **lift, elevator** | l'ascenseur | *lassONsser* |
| **lounge** | le salon | *salON* |
| **lunch** | le déjeuner | *day-juhnay* |
| **manager** | le directeur | *deerekter* |
| **receipt** | le reçu | *ruh-sOO* |
| **reception** | la réception | *rayssep-siON* |
| **receptionist** | la réceptionniste | *rayssep-sioneest* |
| **restaurant** | le restaurant | *restorON* |
| **room** | la chambre | *shombr* |
| **room service** | le service en chambre | *serveess ON shombr* |
| **shower** | la douche | *doosh* |
| **single room** | une chambre pour une personne | *shombr poor OOn pairson* |
| **toilet** | les toilettes | *twallet* |
| **twin room** | une chambre à deux lits | *shombr ah duh lee* |

**Have you any vacancies?**
Avez-vous des chambres de libres?
*avay voo day shombr duh leebr?*

**I have a reservation**
J'ai réservé
*jay raizairvay*

**I'd like a single room**
Je voudrais une chambre pour une personne
*juh voodreh OOn shombr poor OOn pairson*

**I'd like a double/twin room**
Je voudrais une chambre pour deux personnes/à deux lits
*juh voodreh OOn shombr poor duh pairson/ah duh lee*

**I'd like a room with a bathroom/balcony**
Je voudrais une chambre avec salle de bain/balcon
*juh voodreh OOn shombr avek sal duh bAN/bal-kON*

**I'd like a room for one night/three nights**
Je voudrais une chambre pour une nuit/trois nuits
*juh voodreh OOn shombr poor OOn nwee/trwah nwee*

**What is the charge per night?**
Quel est le prix pour une nuit?
*kell eh luh pree poor OOn nwee?*

---

### REPLIES YOU MAY BE GIVEN

**Je suis désolé, mais nous sommes complets**
I'm sorry we're full

**Nous n'avons plus de chambre pour deux personnes/une personne**
We have no double/single rooms left

**Veuillez payer d'avance**
Please pay in advance

**Les chambres doivent être libérées à...**
You must vacate the room by...

---

**I don't know yet how long I'll stay**
Je ne sais pas encore combien de temps je vais rester
*juh nuh seh paz ONkor kombyON duh tAN juh veh restay*

**When is breakfast/dinner?**
A quelle heure servez-vous le petit déjeuner/dîner?
*ah kell er servay voo luh puhtee day-juhnay/deenay?*

**Would you have my luggage brought up?**
Pouvez-vous monter mes bagages dans la chambre?
*poovay voo mONtay may bagaj dON la shombr?*

**Please call me at ... o'clock**
Réveillez-moi à ..., s'il vous plaît
*rayvay-yay mwah ah ..., seel voo pleh*

**Can I have breakfast in my room?**
Pouvez-vous servir mon petit déjeuner dans la chambre?
*poovay voo serveer mON puhtee day-juhnay dON la shambr?*

**I'll be back at ... o'clock**
Je serai de retour à ...
*juh suhray duh ruhtoor ah*

**My room number is...**
Le numéro de ma chambre est le...
*luh nOOmero duh ma shombr eh luh*

**I'm leaving tomorrow**
Je pars demain
*juh par duhmAN*

**Can I have the bill please?**
Pouvez-vous préparer ma note, s'il vous plaît?
*poovay-voo prayparay ma not, seel voo pleh?*

**Can you get me a taxi?**
Pouvez-vous appeler un taxi?
*poovay voo applay AN taxee?*

**Can you recommend another hotel?**
Pouvez-vous recommander un autre hôtel?
*poovay voo ruhkommONday AN oht-r oh-tell?*

## *THINGS YOU'LL SEE OR HEAR*

| | |
|---|---|
| **Addition** | bill |
| **Ascenseur** | lift |
| **Chambre à deux lits** | twin room |
| **Complet** | no vacancies |
| **Douche** | shower |
| **Entrée** | entrance |
| **Escalier** | stairs |
| **Garage** | garage |
| **Issue de secours** | emergency exit |
| **Lavabo** | washbasin |
| **Pension complète** | full board |
| **Pension de famille** | guest-house |
| **Poussez** | push |
| **Privé** | private |
| **Réception** | reception |
| **Réservé** | reserved |
| **Rez-de-chaussée** | ground floor |
| **Salle de bain** | bathroom |
| **Sortie de secours** | emergency exit |
| **Sous-sol** | basement |
| **Supplément** | supplement |
| **Tirez** | pull |
| **1er étage** | first floor |

# CAMPING & CARAVANNING

There are more than 6,000 recognised camping sites in France. Most of these have an enclosure under constant supervision, running water, washing places, wash houses, hygienic lavatories, a refuse clearance service and facilities for buying food in or near the camp. Full information can be obtained from: Le Camping Club de France, 218 boulevard St-Germain, 75007 Paris, or the Fédération Française de Camping et Caravaning, 78 rue de Rivoli, 75004 Paris.

*Youth Hostels:* there are more than 300 Youth Hostels in France which are available to anybody who holds a YHA membership card. This card can be obtained in the UK and is valid all over the world. Most French hostels provide only the bare essentials. For further information you should consult your own Youth Hostel Association or the Fédération Unie des Auberges de la Jeunesse, 6 rue Mesnil, 75016 Paris, or 10 rue Notre-Dame de Lorette, 75009 Paris, or the Ligue Française pour les Auberges de la Jeunesse, 38 boulevard Raspail, 75007 Paris.

## USEFUL WORDS AND PHRASES

| | | |
|---|---|---|
| **bucket** | un seau | *soh* |
| **campsite** | un terrain de camping | *terrAN duh kompeeng* |
| **campfire** | un feu de camp | *fuh duh kON* |
| **to go camping** | aller camper | *allay kompay* |
| **caravan (R.V.)** | une caravane | *karavan* |
| **caravan site** | une terrain de camping/caravaning | *terrAN duh kompeeng/ karavaneeng* |
| **cooking utensils** | des utensiles de cuisine | *days OOtONseel duh kweezeen* |
| **drinking water** | de l'eau potable | *loh pot-abl* |
| **ground sheet** | un tapis de sol | *tapee duh sol* |
| **to hitch hike** | faire du stop | *fair dOO stop* |
| **rope** | une corde | *kord* |
| **rubbish** | les ordures | *ordOOr* |
| **rucksack** | un sac à dos | *sak ah doh* |
| **saucepans** | des casseroles | *day kassrol* |

| **sleeping bag** | un sac de couchage | *sak duh kooshaj* |
| **tent** | une tente | *tONt* |
| **youth hostel** | une auberge de jeunesse | *oh-berj duh juhness* |

**Can I camp here?**
Puis-je camper ici?
*pweej kompay ee-see?*

**Can we park the caravan (trailer) here?**
Pouvons-nous garer notre caravane ici?
*poovON noo garray notr karavan ee-see?*

**Where is the nearest campsite/caravan site?**
Où se trouve le terrain de camping/caravaning lc plus proche?
*oo suh troov luh terrAN duh kompeeng/karavaneeng luh plOO prosh?*

**What is the charge per night?**
Quel est le prix pour une nuit?
*kell eh luh pree poor OOn nwee?*

**What facilities are there?**
Comment ce terrain est-il équipé?
*kommON suh terrAN etteel aykeepay?*

**Can I light a fire here?**
Est-ce que je peux faire un feu ici?
*esskuh juh puh fair AN fuh ee-see*

**Where can I get...?**
Savez-vous où je peux trouver...?
*sahvay voo oo juh puh troovay*

**Is there drinking water here?**
Y a-t-il de l'eau potable ici?
*ee ateel duh loh pot-abl ee-see?*

## *THINGS YOU'LL SEE OR HEAR*

| | |
|---|---|
| **Allumer** | to light |
| **A louer** | for rent |
| **Auberge de jeunesse** | youth hostel |
| **Camping interdit** | no camping |
| **Caravane** | caravan, trailer (R.V.) |
| **Couverture** | blanket |
| **Cuisine** | kitchen |
| **Douches** | showers |
| **Eau non potable** | not drinking water |
| **Eau potable** | drinking water |
| **Emplacement** | site |
| **Entrée** | entrance |
| **Feu** | fire |
| **Gérant** | manager |
| **Lampe** | lamp |
| **Lampe de poche** | torch |
| **Lumière** | light |
| **Piquet** | peg |
| **Réchaud à gaz** | calor gas stove |
| **Recharge** | refill |
| **Remorque** | trailer |
| **Sac de couchage** | sleeping bag |
| **Sanitaires** | toilets/showers |
| **Tente** | tent |
| **Terrain de camping** | camping site |
| **Toile de tente** | tent |
| **Toilettes** | toilet |

# MOTORING

*Rules of the road:* Drive on the right, overtake on the left.

A solid line in the centre of the road must never be crossed. A broken central line may be crossed for the purpose of overtaking another vehicle or crossing the road. Double lines, one continuous and the other broken, may be crossed only where the broken line is immediately to the driver's left. Double lines must not be crossed when the continuous line is nearest to the driver's left-hand side.

To turn right at a crossing, signal and keep as close as possible to the nearside kerb, making a narrow turn. To turn left, go as close as possible to the middle of the road and turn near the centre of the junction, taking care not to enter the new road on the left-hand side!

The use of the horn is very frequent in France (especially in Paris) even if the "code de la route" (highway code) forbids it.

Don't forget that in France, seat belts must be worn at all times.

*Speed limits:* In built-up areas vehicles must not exceed 60 km/h (37 mph). Some urban areas have a lower speed limit than this, which is indicated at the point when it comes into force. Outside urban areas the speed limits are as follows: toll motorways 130 km/h (81 mph); free motorways and multi-lane highways 110 km/h (68 mph); all other roads 90 km/h (56 mph). These apply also to motor bikes over 81cc; lighter machines (51cc-80cc) are restricted to 75 km/h (46 mph) while mopeds up to 50cc may not travel faster than 45 km/h (28 mph). On wet roads, speed limits are reduced from 130 to 110 km/h, from 110 to 100 km/h and from 90 to 80 km/h.

*Right of way:* In built-up areas you must give way to vehicles coming out of a turning on your right. On some roundabouts you may have priority, or you may see a sign saying *Vous n'avez pas la priorité* (below the usual roundabout symbol in a red triangle) – meaning you must give way. Outside built-up areas, your priority is indicated by *Passage protégé* below a cross-roads sign, or by the familiar broad arrow cross-roads sign, or by a yellow diamond sign.

*Parking:* Drivers must park on the right hand side of the road in the direction the car is travelling.

In towns, parking is usually restricted between 9am and 12.30pm and 2.30pm and 7pm during week days. In these zones, the use of a "disque de stationnement" (card showing time of arrival and latest time of departure) displayed inside the windscreen is obligatory. They can be obtained at the Préfecture de Police, at Commissariats de Police or from Motor Clubs.

*Motorways:* There are two types of motorways in France: the "autoroutes de dégagement" which are found around towns and are free, and the "autoroutes de liaison" or "autoroutes à péage" which are toll motorways. The French motorways network is well spread all over the country and allows quick access to most French "régions". The most important are: *l'autoroute du Nord* (Paris-Lille), *l'autoroute de l'Est* (Paris-Strasbourg), *l'autoroute du Soleil* (Paris-Marseilles), *La Languedocienne* (Orange-Le Perthus), *l'Aquitaine* (Paris-Bordeaux) and *l'Océane* (Paris-Nantes).

---

### *SOME COMMON ROAD SIGNS*
The majority of road signs in France are easy to recognise, they usually show diagrams which are very easy to understand.

| | |
|---|---|
| **Accotement non stabilisé** | soft verge |
| **Autoroute** | motorway |
| **Autoroute à péage** | toll motorway |
| **Carrefour dangereux** | dangerous crossroads |
| **Chaussée déformée** | uneven road surface |
| **Chaussée glissante** | slippery road |
| **Chute de pierres** | falling rocks |
| **Danger de verglas** | black ice |
| **Déviation** | diversion |
| **Essence** | fuel |
| **Passage à niveau** | level crossing |
| **Passage interdit** | no thoroughfare |
| **Passage protégé** | priority road |
| **Péage** | toll |

| | |
|---|---|
| **Piétons** | pedestrians |
| **Ralentir** | slow down |
| **Rappel** | reminder (on road signs) |
| **Riverains autorisés** | residents only |
| **Route barrée** | road closed |
| **Route départementale** | secondary road |
| **Route nationale** | main road |
| **Route verglassée** | black ice |
| **Sortie** | exit |
| **Stationnement alterné** | parking on alternate sides |
| **Stationnement interdit** | no parking |
| **Travaux** | men at work |
| **Virage dangereux** | dangerous bend |
| **Virages sur ... km** | bends for ... km |

## USEFUL WORDS AND PHRASES

| | | |
|---|---|---|
| **bonnet** | le capot | *kapo* |
| **boot** | le coffre | *koffr* |
| **brake** | les freins | *frAN* |
| **breakdown** | une panne | *pan* |
| **car** | la voiture | *vwahtOOr* |
| **caravan** | la caravane | *karavan* |
| **crossroads** | un carrefour | *karrfoor* |
| **to drive** | conduire | *kONdweer* |
| **engine** | le moteur | *moter* |
| **exhaust** | le pot d'échappement | *poh dayshappmON* |
| **fanbelt** | la courroie du | *koorwah dOO* |
| | ventilateur | *vONteelatter* |
| **garage (repairs)** | un garage | *garraj* |
| (for fuel) | une station-service | *stassiON serveess* |
| **gasoline** | l'essence | *lessONss* |
| **gear** | la vitesse | *veetess* |
| **gear box** | la boîte de vitesse | *bwat duh veetess* |
| **hood** | le capot | *kapo* |

| indicator | le clignotant | *kleen-yotON* |
|---|---|---|
| junction (on motorway) | un embranchement | *ombrANshmON* |
| licence | le permis de conduire | *permee duh kONdweer* |
| lights (head) | les phares | *far* |
| (rear) | les feux arrière | *fuh arree-air* |
| lorry | le camion | *kamiON* |
| mirror | le rétroviseur | *retroveezer* |
| motorbike | la moto | *moto* |
| motorway | l'autoroute | *lohto-root* |
| number plate | la plaque d'immatriculation | *plak deematreekOO-lassiON* |
| petrol | l'essence | *lessONss* |
| plug | une bougie | *boojee* |
| road | la route | *root* |
| skid | déraper | *dayrappay* |
| spares | des pièces de rechange | *day pee-ess duh ruhshONj* |
| speed | la vitesse | *veetess* |
| speed limit | vitesse limitée | *veetess leemeetay* |
| speedometer | le compteur de vitesse | *kONter duh veetess* |
| steering wheel | le volant | *volAN* |
| tire, tyre | un pneu | *p-nuh* |
| to tow | remorquer | *ruhmorkay* |
| traffic lights | les feux | *fuh* |
| trailer | une remorque | *ruhmork* |
| trailer (R.V.) | la caravane | *karavan* |
| truck | un camion | *kamiON* |
| trunk | le coffre | *koffr* |
| van | la camionnette | *kamionet* |
| wheel | la roue | *roo* |
| windscreen/ shield | le pare-brise | *par breez* |

**I'd like some fuel/oil/water**
Je voudrais de l'essence/de l'huile/de l'eau
*juh voodreh duh lessONss/duh lweel/duh loh*

**Fill her up please**
Le plein, s'il vous plaît
*luh plAN seel voo pleh*

**I'd like 10 litres of petrol/gas**
Je voudrais dix litres d'essence
*juh voodreh dee leetr dessONss*

**How do I get to...?**
Comment puis-je me rendre à...?
*kommON pweej muh rONdr ah?*

**Is this the road to...?**
Est-ce que c'est la route pour...?
*esskuh seh la root poor?*

**Where is the nearest garage?**
Pouvez-vous m'indiquer le garage le plus proche?
*poovay voo mANdeekay luh garraj luh ploo prosh?*

---

### DIRECTIONS YOU MAY BE GIVEN

| | |
|---|---|
| **A droite** | right |
| **A gauche** | left |
| **Au prochain carrefour** | at the next crossroads |
| **Avancez** | go forward |
| **Deuxième à gauche** | second on the left |
| **Passez...** | go past... |
| **Première à droite** | first on the right |
| **Reculez** | reverse |
| **Tournez à droite** | turn right |
| **Tournez à gauche** | turn left |
| **Tout droit** | straight on |

**Would you check the tires please?**
Pouvez-vous vérifier la pression des pneus?
*poovay voo vayreefee-ay la press-iON day p-nuh?*

**Do you do repairs?**
Faites-vous les réparations?
*fet voo lay rayparassiON?*

**Can you repair the clutch?**
Pouvez-vous réparer l'embrayage?
*poovay voo rayparay lombrayaj?*

**How long will it take?**
Combien de temps est-ce que ça prendra?
*kombyAN duh tON esskuh sah prONdra?*

**There is something wrong with the engine**
Le moteur ne fonctionne pas bien
*luh moter nuh fONksi-on pa byAN*

**The engine is overheating**
Le moteur chauffe
*luh moter shofe*

**I need a new tire**
Je voudrais un pneu neuf
*juh voodreh AN p-nuh nuhf*

**Where can I park?**
Où puis-je me garer?
*oo pweej muh garray?*

**Can I park here?**
Est-ce que je peux me garer ici?
*esskuh juh puh muh garray ee-see?*

**I'd like to hire a car**
Je voudrais louer une voiture
*juh voodreh loo-ay OOn vwahtOOr*

---

### *THINGS YOU'LL SEE OR HEAR*

| | |
|---|---|
| **Aire de repos** | rest area |
| **Aire de service** | services area |
| **Arrêt interdit** | no stopping |
| **Brouillard fréquent** | fog |
| **Changer de file** | change lane |
| **Dépanneuse** | breakdown van |
| **Embouteillage** | traffic jam |
| **Essence** | petrol, gasoline |
| **Essuie-glace** | windscreen wiper |
| **Eteignez votre moteur** | switch off engine |
| **Fin de l'autoroute** | end of motorway |
| **Montant exact** | exact change |
| **Niveau d'huile** | oil level |
| **Normale** | two-star petrol, gasoline |
| **Prenez un ticket** | take a ticket |
| **Pression des pneus** | tire pressure |
| **Roulez au' pas** | drive at walking speed |
| **Super** | four-star petrol, gasoline |
| **Station-service** | filling station |

---

# RAIL TRAVEL

The French railways (SNCF) are both fast and punctual, and have two classes, first and second. International trains connect Paris with most parts of Europe, while fast, regular Inter-City and express services link the main French towns. The main types of train are:

TEE: Trans-Europe Express.

TGV (Train à Grande Vitesse): High-speed train.

Rapide: fast Inter-City train, often named (l'Aquitaine, le Drapeau, l'Entendard, le Mistral etc). The rolling stock on Rapide trains is being replaced by very comfortable 'Corail' coaches.

Express: an ordinary fast train.

A supplement is payable for all journeys by TEE and Rapide trains, and booking is essential on the TGV train. If you buy any rail ticket in France (rather than book it before you get there), you must validate this by inserting it into one of the orange-coloured machines at the platform entrance. If you don't date-stamp it like this, you may be fined by a roving ticket inspector.

## USEFUL WORDS AND PHRASES

| | | |
|---|---|---|
| **booking office** | le guichet | *gheeshay* |
| **buffet** | le buffet de la gare | *bOOfay duh la gar* |
| **carriage, car** | la voiture | *vwahtOOr* |
| **compartment** | le compartiment | *komparteemON* |
| **connection** | la correspondance | *korreh-spON-dONss* |
| **currency exchange** | le change | *shONj* |
| **dining car** | la voiture de restauration | *vwahtOOr duh rest-oh-rassiON* |
| **emergency cord** | la sonnette d'alarme | *sonnet dallarm* |
| **engine** | la locomotive | *lokomoteev* |
| **entrance** | l'entrée | *ONtray* |
| **exit** | la sortie | *sortee* |
| **first class** | première classe | *pruhmee-air klass* |
| **to get in** | monter | *mONtay* |

| | | |
|---|---|---|
| **to get out** | descendre | *duhssONdr* |
| **guard** | le chef de train | *shef duh trAN* |
| **indicator board** | le panneau d'affichage | *panno daffee-shaj* |
| **left luggage** | la consigne | *konseen* |
| **lost property** | les objets trouvés | *objay troovay* |
| **luggage locker** | la consigne | *konseen* |
| | automatique | *ott-omateek* |
| **luggage rack** | le porte-bagages | *port bagaj* |
| **luggage trolley** | un chariot | *sharee-o* |
| **luggage van** | un fourgon | *foorgON* |
| **platform** | le quai | *kay* |
| **railways** | les chemins de fer | *shuhmAN duh fair* |
| **reserved seat** | place réservée | *plass rayzairvay* |
| **restaurant car** | le wagon-restaurant | *vagON restorON* |
| **return ticket** | un aller-retour | *allay-ruhtoor* |
| **seat** | une place | *plass* |
| **second class** | seconde | *segONd* |
| **single ticket** | un aller simple | *allay samp-l* |
| **sleeping car** | le wagon-lit | *vagON lee* |
| **station** | la gare | *gar* |
| **station master** | le chef de gare | *shef duh gar* |
| **ticket** | un billet | *bee-yay* |
| **ticket collector** | le contrôleur | *kontroler* |
| **timetable** | l'horaire | *lorrair* |
| **tracks** | les rails | *rah-ee* |
| **train** | le train | *trAN* |
| **waiting room** | la salle d'attente | *sal dattONt* |
| **window** | la fenêtre | *fuhn-ettr* |

**When does the train for ... leave?**
A quelle heure part le train pour...?
*ah kell er par luh trAN poor?*

**When does the train from ... arrive?**
A quelle heure arrive le train en provenance de...?
*ah kell er arreev luh trAN ON provnONss duh?*

**When is the next/first/last train to…?**
A quelle heure part le prochain/premier/dernier train pour…?
*a kell er par luh proshAN/pruhmee-ay/dairnee-ay trAN poor?*

**What is the fare to…?**
Quel est le prix du billet pour…?
*kell eh luh pree dOO bee-yay poor?*

**Do I have to change?**
Faut-il que je change de train?
*fo-teel kuh juh shONj duh trAN?*

**Does the train stop at…?**
Est-ce que le train s'arrête à…?
*esskuh luh trAN sarret ah?*

**How long does it take to get to…?**
Combien de temps faut-il pour aller à…?
*kombyAN duh tON fo-teel poor allay ah …?*

---

*REPLIES YOU MAY BE GIVEN:*

**Il n'y a que des premières dans ce train**
There is only first class on this train

**Vous devez payer un supplément**
You have to pay a supplement

**Le train suivant est à…**
The next train is at…

**Changez à…**
Change at…

**A single/return ticket to ... please**
Un aller simple/aller-retour pour ..., s'il vous plaît
*AN allay samp-l/allay-ruhtoor poor ... seel voo pleh*

**Do I have to pay a supplement?**
Est-ce qu'il y a un supplément à payer?
*esskeel-ya AN sOOplaymON ah payay?*

**I'd like to reserve a seat**
Je voudrais réserver une place
*juh voodreh rayzairvay OOn plass*

**Is this the right train for...?**
Est-ce bien le train pour...?
*ess byAN luh trAN poor?*

**Is this the right platform for the ... train?**
Est-ce bien le quai pour le train qui va à...?
*ess byAN luh kay poor luh trAN kee va ah?*

**Which platform for the ... train?**
Sur quel quai part le train pour...?
*sOOr kell kay par luh trAN poor?*

**Is the train late?**
Est-ce que le train a du retard?
*esskuh luh trAN ah dOO ruhtar?*

**Could you help me with my luggage please?**
Pouvez-vous m'aider à porter mes bagages, s'il vous plaît?
*poovay voo mehday ah portay may bagaj, seel voo pleh?*

**Is this a non-smoking compartment?**
Ce compartiment est-il non fumeurs?
*suh kompartee-mON eteel nON fOOmer?*

**Is this seat free?**
Est-ce que cette place est libre?
*esskuh set plass eh leebr?*

**This seat is taken**
Cette place est occupée
*set plass et okkOOpay*

**I have reserved this seat**
J'ai réservé cette place
*jay rayzairvay set plass*

**May I open/close the window?**
Est-ce que je peux ouvrir/fermer la fenêtre?
*esskuh juh puh oovreer/fairmay la fuhn-ettr?*

**When do we arrive in...?**
Savez-vous à quelle heure nous arrivons à...?
*sahvay voo ah kell er nooz arreevON ah?*

**What station is this?**
Quelle est cette gare?
*kell eh set gar?*

**When does my connection leave?**
A quelle heure part la correspondance?
*ah kell er par lah korrehspondONss?*

**Do we stop at...?**
Est-ce que le train s'arrête à...?
*esskuh luh trAN sarret ah?*

**Would you keep an eye on my things for a moment?**
Pouvez-vous surveiller mes affaires pendant un moment?
*poovay voo sOOrvay-yay maiz affair pONdON AN momON?*

**Is there a restaurant car on this train?**
Est-ce qu'il y a une voiture de restauration dans ce train?
*esskeel-ya OOn vwatOOr duh restorassiON dON suh trAN?*

## *THINGS YOU'LL SEE OR HEAR*

| | |
|---|---|
| Accès aux trains | to the trains |
| Accès aux quais | to the platforms |
| Amende | fine |
| Arrivée(s) | arrival(s) |
| Attention au départ | the train is about to leave |
| Banlieues | suburban services |
| Billets | tickets |
| Bureau d'accueil | reception centre |
| Change | exchange |
| Climatisation | air conditioning |
| Climatisé | with air conditioning |
| Compartiment fumeurs | smoking compartment |
| Compartiment non fumeurs | non smoking compartment |
| Composition du train | order of cars |
| Composter | to punch (tickets) |
| Consigne | left luggage |
| Consigne automatique | luggage lockers |
| Couchette | sleeper with bunk bed |
| Départ(s) | departure(s) |
| Descendre | to get off |
| Desservir | to stop at |
| Dimanche et jours fériés | on Sundays and public holidays |
| Distributeur de billets | ticket machine |
| Entrée | entrance |
| Entrée interdite | no entry |
| Fermé | closed |
| Fumeurs | smoking |
| Gare | station |
| Hall de départ | departure hall |
| Hall d'arrivée | arrival hall |
| Hall de gare | station hall |
| Horaires | timetable |
| Interdiction de marcher sur la voie | do not walk on the track |

→

| | |
|---|---|
| **Le train dessert les gares de...** | the train will stop at... |
| **Le train va entrer en gare** | the train is about to arrive |
| **Libre** | free |
| **Monter** | to get in |
| **Non fumeurs** | no smoking |
| **N'oubliez pas de composter votre billet** | don't forget to validate your ticket |
| **Occupé** | engaged |
| **Passage sous-terrain** | underground passage |
| **Première** | first class |
| **Privé** | private |
| **Quai** | platform |
| **Renseignements** | enquiries |
| **Réservé** | reserved |
| **Restauration à la place** | meal served at your seat (1st class only) |
| **Salle d'attente** | waiting room |
| **Sans issue** | no way out |
| **Seconde** | second class |
| **Sonnette d'alarme** | communication cord |
| **Tarif** | price |
| **Ticket de quai** | platform ticket |
| **Toilettes** | toilet |
| **Tous les jours sauf...** | every day except on... |
| **Train à supplément** | train with supplement |
| **Voiture** | coach, car |
| **Voiture de restauration** | dining car |
| **Voyage** | trip |
| **Voyageur** | traveller |
| **Wagon-lit** | sleeper-car |

# AIR TRAVEL

Paris has two international airports, Orly and Charles-de-Gaulle at Roissy. Both are connected to the main terminals and rail stations in Paris by bus (navettes), and there's also a train service to Charles-de-Gaulle.

## USEFUL WORDS AND PHRASES

| | | |
|---|---|---|
| **aircraft** | l'appareil | *lapparay* |
| **air hostess** | l'hôtesse (de l'air) | *lottess (duh lair)* |
| **airline** | la compagnie aérienne | *kompan-yee ah-ayree-enne* |
| **airport** | l'aéroport | *lah-ayropor* |
| **airport bus** | la navette de l'aéroport | *navet duh lah-ayropor* |
| **arrival** | l'arrivée | *larrevay* |
| **baggage claim** | retrait des bagages | *ruhtray day bagaj* |
| **boarding card** | la carte d'embarquement | *kart dombarkemON* |
| **check-in** | enregistrement | *ONruhjeestruh-mON* |
| **check-in desk** | enregistrement des bagages | *ONruhjeestruh-mON day bagaj* |
| **delay** | du retard | *dOO ruhtar* |
| **departure** | le départ | *daypar* |
| **departure lounge** | la salle d'embarquement | *sal dombarkemON* |
| **emergency exit** | sortie de secours | *sortee duh suh-koor* |
| **flight** | le vol | *vol* |
| **flight number** | le numéro du vol | *nOOmero dOO vol* |
| **gate** | la porte | *port* |
| **jet** | un jet | *jet* |
| **landing** | l'atterrissage | *attaireessaj* |
| **passport** | un passeport | *passpor* |

| | | |
|---|---|---|
| **passport control** | contrôle des passeports | *kontroll day passpor* |
| **pilot** | le pilote | *peelot* |
| **runway** | la piste | *peest* |
| **seat** | une place | *plass* |
| **seat belt** | la ceinture | *sANtOOr* |
| **steward** | le steward | |
| **stewardess** | l'hôtesse | *lottess* |
| **take off** | le décollage | *daykollaj* |
| **window** | le hublot | *OOblo* |
| **wing** | l'aile | *el* |

**When is there a flight to...?**
A quelle heure y a-t-il un vol pour...?
*ah kell er ee-ateel AN vol poor?*

**What time does the flight to... leave?**
A quelle heure part le vol pour...?
*ah kell er par luh vol poor?*

**Is it a direct flight?**
Est-ce un vol direct?
*ess AN vol deerekt?*

**Do I have to change planes?**
Faut-il prendre une correspondance?
*fo-teel prONdr OOn korrehspONdONss?*

**When do I have to check in?**
A quelle heure dois-je me présenter à l'enregistrement?
*ah kell er dwaj muh praysONtay ah lONruhjeestruhmON?*

**I'd like a single/return ticket to...**
Je voudrais un aller simple/un aller-retour pour...
*juh voodreh AN allay samp-l/AN allay-ruhtoor poor*

**I'd like a non-smoking seat please**
Je voudrais une place en non fumeurs, s'il vous plaît
*juh voodreh OOn plass ON nON fOOmer seel voo pleh*

**I'd like a window seat please**
Je voudrais une place à côté du hublot, s'il vous plaît
*juh voodreh OOh plass ah kotay dOO OOblo seel voo pleh*

**How long will the flight be delayed?**
Combien l'avion aura-t-il de retard?
*kombyAN laviON oh-ratteel duh ruhtar?*

**Is this the right gate for the ... flight?**
Est-ce que c'est la bonne porte pour le ... vol de?
*esskuh seh la bon port poor luh vol duh?*

**When do we arrive in...?**
A quelle heure arrivons-nous à...?
*ah kell er arreevON noo ah?*

**May I smoke now?**
Est-ce que je peux fumer maintenant?
*esskuh juh puh fOOmay mentnON*

**I do not feel very well**
Je ne me sens pas très bien
*juh nuh muh sON pa treh byAN*

---

### THINGS YOU'LL SEE OR HEAR

| | |
|---|---|
| **Altitude** | altitude |
| **Arrivée** | arrival |
| **Attachez vos ceintures** | fasten your seat belt |
| **Atterrissage** | landing |

$\longrightarrow$

| | |
|---|---|
| **Atterrissage forcé** | emergency landing |
| **Contrôle des passeports** | passport control |
| **Contrôle des bagages** | luggage control |
| **Départ** | departure |
| **Embarquement** | boarding |
| **Embarquement immédiat** | boarding now |
| **Enregistrement des bagages** | check-in desk |
| **Enregistrer** | to check-in |
| **Escale** | stop-over |
| **Fumeurs** | smoking |
| **Heure** | time |
| **Horaire** | timetable |
| **Hôtesse** | air hostess |
| **Informations** | enquiries |
| **Issue de secours** | emergency exit |
| **Non fumeurs** | no smoking |
| **Passager(s)** | passenger(s) |
| **Piste** | runway |
| **Police de l'aéroport** | airport police |
| **Poussez** | push |
| **Porte** | door/gate |
| **Relevez** | lift up |
| **Réservé aux membres de l'équipage** | reserved for the crew |
| **Retard** | delay |
| **Retardé** | late |
| **Retrait des bagages** | luggage claim |
| **Satellite** | section of airport terminal |
| **Sortie de secours** | emergency exit |
| **Tirez** | pull |
| **Vitesse** | speed |
| **Vol** | flight |
| **Vol direct** | direct flight |

# METRO, BUS & TAXI TRAVEL

In Paris, the "métro" (underground tube train or subway) is the fastest and most economical way to travel. It's a one-price service regardless of distance, and trains run from about 5.30am to 12.30am. Tickets are cheapest when bought in booklets of ten (carnets), and you can also buy special tourist tickets (enquire at métro or railway stations, or at any Office de Tourisme in Paris). Lille, Lyon and Marseille also have métro systems.

In the country, buses link mainline railway stations with most towns and villages not served by trains. Tickets are available at newsagents (tabac-journaux) and – as in Paris, where the same tickets or passes can be used either on the métro or on the bus – fares are calculated by distance, one ticket for one fare stage. There are also long-distance coaches and a considerable number of sight-seeing tours.

Taxis are clearly marked and can be hailed or picked up at a rank (there's usually one at the train station). If the cab has no meter, or if you are going some distance out of town, check the fare beforehand.

## USEFUL WORDS AND PHRASES

| | | |
|---|---|---|
| **adult** | un adulte | *adOOlt* |
| **bus** | un bus | *bOOs* |
| **bus stop** | un arrêt de bus | *array duh bOOs* |
| **child** | un enfant | *ONFON* |
| **coach** | un car | *kar* |
| **connection** | la correspondance | *korrehspONdONss* |
| **driver** | le conducteur | *kondOOkter* |
| **fare** | le prix du ticket | *pree dOO teekay* |
| **network map** | un plan du réseau | *plON dOO rayzo* |
| **number 5 bus** | le bus numéro 5 | *bOOs nOOmero 5* |
| **passenger** | un passager | *passajay* |
| **seat** | une place | *plass* |
| **station** | la station | *stassiON* |
| **taxi** | un taxi | *taxi* |

| **terminus** | le terminus | *termeenOOs* |
| **ticket** | le ticket | *teekay* |
| **underground, subway** | le métro | *maytro* |

**Where is the nearest underground station?**
Pouvez-vous m'indiquer la station de métro la plus proche?
*poovay voo mANdeekay la stassiON duh maytro la plOO prosh?*

**Where is the bus station?**
Où se trouve la gare routière?
*oo suh troov la gar rootee-air?*

**Where is there a bus stop?**
Où est-ce que je peux trouver un arrêt de bus?
*oo esskuh juh puh troovay AN array duh bOOs?*

**Which buses go to...?**
Quels sont les bus qui vont à...?
*kell sON lay bOOs kee vON ah?*

**How often do the buses to ... run?**
Quelle est la fréquence des bus pour...?
*kell eh la fraikONss day bOOs poor?*

**Would you tell me when we get to...?**
Pouvez-vous me dire quand nous arrivons à...?
*poovay voo muh deer kAN nooz arreevON ah?*

**Do I have to get off yet?**
Faut-il que je descende maintenant?
*fo-teel kuh juh daysOND mentnON?*

**How do you get to...?**
Comment peut-on se rendre à...?
*kommON puhtON suh rONdr ah?*

**Is it very far?**
C'est très loin?
*seh treh lwAN?*

**I want to go to...**
Je veux aller à...
*juh vuh allay ah*

**Do you go near...?**
Passez-vous près de...?
*passay voo preh duh?*

**Where can I buy a ticket?**
Où est-ce que je peux acheter un ticket?
*oo esskuh juh puh ashtay AN teekay?*

**Please close/open the window**
Pouvez-vous fermer/ouvrir la fenêtre, s'il vous plaît?
*poovay voo fairmay/oovreer la fuhn-ettr seel voo pleh*

**Could you help me get a ticket?**
Pouvez-vous m'aider à acheter un ticket?
*poovay voo mehday a ashtay AN teekay?*

**When does the last bus leave?**
A quelle heure part le dernier bus?
*ah kell er par luh dairnee-ay bOOs*

**Where can I get a taxi from?**
Où puis-je prendre un taxi?
*oo pweej prONdr AN taxi?*

**Please stop here**
Arrêtez-vous ici, s'il vous plaît
*arrettay vooz ee-see, seel voo pleh*

**I'd like a receipt please.**
Je voudrais un reçu, s'il vous plaît
*juh voodrez AN ruhsOO seel voo pleh*

---

### *THINGS YOU'LL SEE OR HEAR*

| | |
|---|---|
| **Amende** | fine |
| **Appuyez ici** | press here |
| **Carte** | pass |
| **Carte de réduction** | reduced-rate ticket |
| **Changement** | change |
| **Changer à...** | change at... |
| **Conservez votre ticket** | keep your ticket |
| **Contrôleur** | inspector |
| **Debout** | standing |
| **Destination** | destination |
| **Direction** | direction |
| **Distributeur de tickets** | ticket machine |
| **Fermé** | closed |
| **Fermeture automatique des portes** | door closes automatically |
| **Interdiction de cracher** | no spitting |
| **Interdiction de fumer** | no smoking |
| **Interdiction de parler au conducteur** | do not speak to the driver |
| **Introduire ici** | insert here |
| **Monter** | to get in |
| **Marche** | step |
| **Ouvert** | open |
| **Ouverture** | opening |
| **Passage interdit** | no entry |
| **Payer** | to pay |
| **Place** | seat |
| **Place(s) assise(s)** | seat(s) |

| | |
|---|---|
| **Plan** | map |
| **Plan du métro** | underground/subway (métro) map |
| **Plan du réseau** | network map (bus/métro) |
| **Pièce(s)** | coin(s) |
| **Pièces rejetées** | reject coins |
| **Poinçonner** | to punch |
| **Première classe** | first class |
| **Privé** | private |
| **Quai** | platform |
| **Rame** | train |
| **Réduction** | reduced rate |
| **Réservé** | reserved |
| **Réservé au personnel** | staff only |
| **Resquilleur** | fare dodger |
| **Station** | station |
| **Station de métro** | tube/subway station |
| **Sortie** | exit |
| **Ticket** | ticket |
| **Titre de transport** | ticket |
| **Trajet** | route |

# RESTAURANT

Here is a list of basic words you'll need. There is a more comprehensive menu guide at the end of this section.

| beer | de la bière | *duh la bee-air* |
|------|-------------|-----------------|
| bill | l'addition | *laddeessiON* |
| bottle | une bouteille | *bootay* |
| bowl | un bol | *boll* |
| bread | du pain | *pAN* |
| butter | du beurre | *ber* |
| cake | un gâteau | *gatto* |
| chef | le chef | *shef* |
| coffee | du café | *kaffay* |
| cup | une tasse | *tass* |
| glass | un verre | *vair* |
| fork | une fourchette | *foorshet* |
| knife | un couteau | *kooto* |
| menu | le menu | *muhnOO* |
| milk | du lait | *leh* |
| plate | une assiette | *assee-et* |
| sandwich | un sandwich | *sONndweetch* |
| serviette | une serviette | *servee-et* |
| snack | un snack | *snack* |
| soup | la soupe | *soop* |
| spoon | une cuillère | *kwee-yair* |
| table | une table | *tabb-l* |
| tea | du thé | *tay* |
| teaspoon | une cuillère à café | *kwee-yair ah kaffay* |
| tip | un pourboire | *poorbwahr* |
| waiter | un serveur | *sairver* |
| waitress | une serveuse | *sairvuhz* |
| water | de l'eau | *loh* |
| wine | du vin | *vAN* |
| wine list | la carte des vins | *kart day vAN* |

**A table for one/two/three please**
Une table pour une/deux/trois personnes, s'il vous plaît
*OOn tabl poor OOn/duh/trwah pairson, seel voo pleh*

**I only want a snack**
Je voudrais juste manger un snack
*juh voodreh jOOst mONjay AN snack*

**I just want a cup of coffee/tea**
Un café/thé seulement
*AN kaffay/tay suhlmON*

**Can we see the menu/wine list?**
Pouvez-vous nous donner le menu/la carte des vins?
*poovay voo noo donnay luh muhnOO/la kart day vAN?*

**Is there a set menu?**
Y a-t-il un menu du jour?
*ee ateel AN muhnOO dOO joor?*

**What would you recommend?**
Que recommandez-vous?
*kuh ruhkommONday voo?*

**I'd like...**
Je voudrais...
*juh voodreh*

**Waiter!**
Garçon!
*garssON*

**We didn't order this**
Ce n'est pas ce que nous avons commandé
*sneh pa suh kuh nooz avON kommONday*

**May we have some more...?**
Est-ce qu'on peut avoir plus de...?
*esskON puh avwarr plOOs duh?*

**Can we have the bill please?**
L'addition, s'il vous plaît
*laddeessiON seel voo pleh*

**Could I have a receipt please?**
Est-ce que je peux avoir un reçu, s'il vous plaît?
*esskuh juh puh avwarr AN ruhsOO, seel voo pleh?*

**The meal was very good, thank you**
Le repas était très bon, merci
*luh ruhpa ayteh treh bON, mairsee*

**My compliments to the chef!**
Veuillez complimenter le chef de ma part
*vuh-yay kompleemONtay luh shef duh ma par*

## *MENU GUIDE*

| | |
|---|---|
| à la normande | in cream sauce |
| à la provençale | with tomatoes, garlic and herbs |
| à point | well done |
| abats | offal |
| abricot | apricot |
| agneau | lamb |
| aiguillette de boeuf | slices of rump steak |
| ail | garlic |
| ailloli | garlic mayonnaise |
| alose | shad *(type of fish)* |
| amande | almond |
| ananas | pineapple |
| andouillette | spicy sausage |
| anguille | eel |
| appellation d'origine contrôlée | proof of origin and quality |
| araignée de mer | spider crab |
| artichaut | artichoke |
| asperge | asparagus |
| aspic de volaille | chicken in aspic |
| assiette anglaise | selection of cold meats |
| au vin blanc | in white wine |
| aubergine | aubergine, eggplant |
| avocat | avocado |
| baba au rhum | rum baba |
| banane | banana |
| bananes flambées | bananas flambéd in brandy |
| barbue | brill *(fish)* |
| bavaroise | light mousse |
| béarnaise | with béarnaise sauce |
| bécasse | woodcock |
| béchamel | béchamel sauce *(milk, butter and flour)* |
| beignet | doughnut |
| beignet aux pommes | apple fritter |
| betterave | beetroot |
| beurre | butter |
| beurre d'anchois | anchovy paste |
| beurre d'estragon | butter with tarragon |
| beurre noir | dark melted butter |

| | |
|---|---|
| **bien cuit** | well done |
| **bière** | beer |
| **bière blonde** | lager |
| **bière brune** | bitter, dark beer |
| **bière panachée** | shandy |
| **bifteck** | steak |
| **bifteck de cheval** | horsemeat steak |
| **biscuit de Savoie** | sponge cake |
| **bisque d'écrevisses** | crayfish soup |
| **bisque de homard** | lobster bisque |
| **blanc** | white wine |
| **blanc de blancs** | white wine from white grapes |
| **blanquette de Limoux** | sparkling white wine |
| **blanquette de veau** | veal stew |
| **bleu** | rare |
| **bleu d'Auvergne** | blue cheese from the Auvergne |
| **bœuf** | beef |
| **bœuf à la ficelle** | beef cooked in stock |
| **bœuf bourguignon** | beef cooked in red wine |
| **bœuf braisé** | braised beef |
| **bœuf en daube** | beef casserole |
| **bœuf miroton** | beef and onion stew |
| **bœuf mode** | beef stew with carrots |
| **bolet** | boletus *(mushroom)* |
| **bouchée à la reine** | vol-au-vent |
| **boudin** | black pudding |
| **boudin blanc** | white pudding |
| **bouillabaisse** | fish soup from the Midi |
| **bouillon** | broth |
| **bouillon de légumes** | vegetable soup |
| **bouillon de poule** | chicken stock |
| **boulette** | meatball |
| **bouquet rose** | prawns |
| **bourride** | fish soup |
| **braisé** | braised |
| **brandade** | cod in cream and garlic |
| **brioche** | round bun |
| **brochet** | pike |
| **brochette** | kebab |
| **brugnon** | nectarine |
| **brûlot** | flambéd brandy |

| | |
|---|---|
| **cabillaud** | cod |
| **café** | coffee (black) |
| **café au lait** | white coffee |
| **café complet** | continental breakfast |
| **café crème** | white coffee |
| **café glacé** | iced coffee |
| **café liégois** | iced coffee with cream |
| **caille** | quail |
| **cake** | fruit cake |
| **calmar** | squid |
| **calvados** | apple brandy from Normandy |
| **camomille** | camomile tea |
| **canapé** | small open sandwich, canapé |
| **canard** | duck |
| **canard à l'orange** | duck in orange sauce |
| **canard aux cerises** | duck with cherries |
| **canard aux navets** | duck with turnips |
| **canard laqué** | Pekin duck |
| **canard rôti** | roast duck |
| **caneton** | duckling |
| **cantal** | cheese from the Auvergne |
| **capiteux** | heady *(wine)* |
| **carbonnade** | beef cooked in beer |
| **cari** | curry |
| **carotte** | carrot |
| **carottes Vichy** | carrots in butter and parsley |
| **carpe** | carp |
| **carrelet** | plaice |
| **carte** | menu |
| **carte des vins** | wine list |
| **cassis** | blackcurrant |
| **cassoulet** | bean, pork and duck casserole |
| **céleri** | celeriac |
| **céleri en branches** | celery |
| **céleri rave** | celeriac |
| **céleri remoulade** | celeriac in mustard dressing |
| **cêpe** | cêpe *(mushroom)* |
| **cerise** | cherry |
| **cerises à l'eau de vie** | cherries in brandy |
| **cervelle** | brains |

| | |
|---|---|
| chabichou | goat and cow's milk cheese |
| Chablis | dry white wine from Burgundy |
| chambré | at room temperature |
| champagne | champagne |
| champignon | mushroom |
| champignon de Paris | champignon *(cultivated mushroom)* |
| champignons à la grecque | mushrooms in olive oil, herbs and tomato |
| chanterelle | chanterelle *(mushroom)* |
| chantilly | whipped cream |
| charcuterie | sausages, ham and pâtés, pork products |
| charlotte | cream with fruit and biscuits |
| chasselas | white grape |
| chausson aux pommes | apple turnover |
| cheval | horse |
| chèvre | goat cheese |
| chevreuil | venison |
| chicorée | endive |
| chiffonnade d'oseille | seasoned sorrel cooked in butter |
| chocolat chaud | hot chocolate |
| chocolat glacé | iced chocolate |
| chocolatine | chocolate puff pastry |
| chou | cabbage |
| chou à la crème | cream puff |
| chou de Bruxelles | Brussels sprout |
| chou rouge | red cabbage |
| chou-fleur | cauliflower |
| chou-fleur au gratin | cauliflower cheese |
| choucroute | sauerkraut |
| cidre bouché | dry cider |
| cidre doux | sweet cider |
| citron | lemon |
| citron pressé | fresh lemon juice |
| civet de lièvre | jugged hare |
| clafoutis | fruit pudding baked in the oven |
| cochon de lait | sucking pig |
| cocktail de crevettes | prawn cocktail |
| cœur | heart |
| coing | quince |

| | |
|---|---|
| colin | hake |
| compote | stewed fruit, compote |
| comté | cheese from the Jura |
| concombre | cucumber |
| confit d'oie | goose preserved in fat |
| confit de canard | duck preserved in fat |
| confiture | jam |
| congre | conger eel |
| coq au vin | chicken in red wine |
| coque | cockle |
| coquelet | cockeral |
| coquille Saint-Jacques | scallop |
| côte de porc | pork chop |
| côtelette | chop |
| cotriade bretonne | fish soup from Brittany |
| coulommiers | rich soft cheese |
| coupe | dessert dish |
| courgette | courgette, zucchini |
| court-bouillon | stock for poaching fish or meat |
| couscous | semolina with meat and vegetable stew |
| crabe | crab |
| crème | cream, creamy sauce or dessert |
| crème à la vanille | vanilla custard |
| crème anglaise | custard |
| crème Chantilly | whipped cream |
| crème d'asperges | cream of asparagus soup |
| crème d'huîtres | cream of oyster soup |
| crème de bolets | cream of mushroom soup |
| crème de volaille | cream of chicken soup |
| crème fouettée | whipped cream |
| crème pâtissière | rich creamy custard |
| crème renversée | set custard |
| crème vichyssoise | cold potato and leek soup |
| crêpe | pancake |
| crêpe à l'œuf | pancake with fried egg |
| crêpe à la béchamel | pancake with béchamel sauce |
| crêpe à la chantilly | pancake with whipped cream |
| crêpe à la confiture | pancake with jam |
| crêpe à la crème de marron | pancake with chestnut cream |
| crêpe au chocolat | pancake with chocolate sauce |

| | |
|---|---|
| **crêpe au jambon** | pancake with ham |
| **crêpe aux fruits de mer** | pancake with seafood |
| **crêpe de froment** | wholemeal flour pancake |
| **crêpes aux champignons** | mushroom pancakes |
| **crêpes aux épinards** | spinach pancakes |
| **crêpes Suzette** | pancakes flambéd with orange |
| **crépinette** | sausage |
| **cresson** | cress |
| **crevette grise** | shrimp |
| **crevette rose** | prawn |
| **croque-Madame** | toasted cheese & ham sandwich with fried egg |
| **croque-Monsieur** | toasted cheese & ham sandwich |
| **crottin de Chavignol** | small goat cheese |
| **crudités** | selection of salads |
| **crustacés** | shellfish |
| **cuisses de grenouille** | frog's legs |
| **cuissot de chevreuil** | haunch of venison |
| **dartois** | pastry with jam |
| **daurade** | gilt-head *(fish)* |
| **dégustation** | (wine) tasting |
| **dégustation de vins** | wine tasting |
| **déjeuner** | lunch |
| **digestif** | liqueur |
| **dinde** | turkey |
| **dîner** | dinner |
| **doux** | sweet |
| **eau minérale** | mineral water |
| **eau minérale gazeuse** | sparkling mineral water |
| **échalote** | shallot |
| **écrevisse** | crayfish |
| **écrevisses à la nage** | crayfish in wine and vegetable sauce |
| **endive** | chicory, endive |
| **endives au jambon** | chicory with ham baked in the oven |
| **endives braisées** | braised chicory |
| **entrecôte** | rib steak |
| **entrecôte au poivre** | rib steak in pepper sauce |
| **entrecôte maître d'hôtel** | rib steak with butter and parsley |
| **entrée** | starter |
| **entremets** | puddings |
| **épaule d'agneau farcie** | stuffed shoulder of lamb |

| | |
|---|---|
| **éperlan** | smelt *(fish)* |
| **épinards à la crème** | spinach with cream |
| **épinards en branches** | leaf spinach |
| **escalope à la crème** | escalope in cream sauce |
| **escalope panée** | breaded escalope |
| **escargot** | snail |
| **esquimau** | ice cream on a stick |
| **estouffade de bœuf** | beef casserole |
| **faisan** | pheasant |
| **farci** | stuffed |
| **fenouil** | fennel |
| **filet** | fillet |
| **filet de bœuf Rossini** | fillet of beef with foie gras |
| **filet de perche** | perch fillet |
| **fine** | fine brandy |
| **flageolet** | kidney bean |
| **flambé** | flambéd |
| **flan** | custard tart |
| **foie de veau** | veal liver |
| **foie gras** | goose or duck liver preserve |
| **foies de volaille** | chicken livers |
| **fonds d'artichaut** | artichoke heart |
| **fondue bourguignonne** | meat fondue |
| **fondue savoyarde** | cheese fondue |
| **fraise** | strawberry |
| **fraise des bois** | wild strawberry |
| **framboise** | raspberry |
| **frisée** | curly lettuce |
| **frit** | deep fried |
| **frites** | chips, French fries |
| **froid** | cold |
| **fromage** | cheese |
| **fromage de chèvre** | goat's cheese |
| **fruité** | fruity |
| **fruits de mer** | seafood |
| **galette** | round flat cake |
| **garni** | with potatoes and vegetables |
| **gâteau** | cake |
| **gaufre** | wafer |
| **gelée** | jelly |
| **génoise** | sponge cake |

| | |
|---|---|
| **Gewurztraminer** | dry white wine from the Alsace |
| **gibelotte de lapin** | rabbit stewed in white wine |
| **gibier** | game |
| **gigot d'agneau** | leg of lamb |
| **gigue de chevreuil** | haunch of venison |
| **girolle** | chanterelle *(mushroom)* |
| **glace** | ice cream |
| **goujon** | gudgeon *(fish)* |
| **grand cru** | vintage wine |
| **gratin** | baked cheese dish |
| **gratin dauphinois** | potato gratin |
| **gratin de langoustines** | crayfish au gratin |
| **gratin de queues d'écrevisse** | crayfish au gratin |
| **gratinée** | baked onion soup with grated cheese |
| **grillé** | grilled |
| **grive** | thrush |
| **grondin** | gurnard *(fish)* |
| **groseille blanche** | white currant |
| **groseille rouge** | red currant |
| **hachis parmentier** | shepherd's pie |
| **hareng mariné** | marinated herring |
| **haricot** | (green) bean |
| **haricot blanc** | haricot bean |
| **haricot de mouton** | mutton stew with beans |
| **haricot vert** | green bean |
| **homard** | lobster |
| **homard à l'américaine** | lobster with tomatoes and white wine |
| **hors-d'œuvre** | starter |
| **huître** | oyster |
| **infusion** | herb tea |
| **jambon** | ham, gammon |
| **jambon au madère** | ham in Madeira wine |
| **jarret de veau** | shin of veal |
| **julienne** | soup with chopped vegetables |
| **jus d'orange** | orange juice |
| **jus de pommes** | apple juice |
| **kir** | white wine with blackcurrant liqueur |
| **kirsch** | cherry brandy |
| **kugelhof** | cake from Alsace |

| | |
|---|---|
| lait | milk |
| lait grenadine | milk with grenadine cordial |
| laitue | lettuce |
| langouste | crayfish |
| langoustine | scampi |
| langue de bœuf | ox tongue |
| lapereau | young rabbit |
| lapin | rabbit |
| lapin à la Lorraine | rabbit in mushroom and cream sauce |
| lapin à la moutarde | rabbit in mustard sauce |
| lapin aux pruneaux | rabbit with prunes |
| lapin de garenne | wild rabbit |
| léger | light |
| légume | vegetable |
| lentille | lentil |
| lièvre | hare |
| limande | dab, lemon sole |
| limonade | lemonade |
| livarot | strong cheese |
| longe | loin |
| lotte | burbot |
| loup au fenouil | bass with fennel |
| macédoine de légumes | mixed vegetables |
| mache | lamb's lettuce |
| mangue | mango |
| maquereau au vin blanc | mackerel in white wine sauce |
| marc | grape brandy |
| marcassin | young wild boar |
| marchand de vin | in wine sauce |
| marinade | marinade |
| marron | chestnut |
| massepain | marzipan |
| melon | melon |
| menthe | peppermint |
| menu gastronomique | gourmet menu |
| menu touristique | tourist menu |
| merlan au vin blanc | whiting in white wine |
| millefeuille | cream slice |
| millésime | vintage |
| morille | morel *(mushroom)* |

| | |
|---|---|
| morue | cod |
| moules à la poulette | mussels in rich white wine sauce |
| moules marinière | mussels in white wine |
| mousse au chocolat | chocolate mousse |
| mousse au jambon | light ham pâté |
| moutarde | mustard |
| mouton | mutton |
| mulet | mullet |
| munster | strong cheese |
| mûre | blackberry |
| Muscadet | dry white wine from Nantes |
| muscat | sweet white wine |
| myrtille | bilberry |
| nature | plain |
| navarin | mutton stew with vegetables |
| navet | turnip |
| noisette | hazelnut |
| noix | walnut |
| nouilles | noodles |
| œuf à la coque | boiled egg |
| œuf dur | hard boiled egg |
| œuf en gelée | egg in aspic |
| œuf mollet | soft-boiled egg |
| œuf poché | poached egg |
| œuf sur le plat | fried egg |
| œufs à la neige | floating islands *(whipped egg white with custard)* |
| œufs brouillés | scrambled eggs |
| oie | goose |
| oignon | onion |
| omelette au fromage | cheese omelette |
| omelette au jambon | ham omelette |
| omelette au naturel | plain omelette |
| omelette aux champignons | mushroom omelette |
| omelette aux fines herbes | omelette with chives |
| omelette aux foies de volaille | omelette with chicken liver |
| omelette paysanne | omelette with potatoes and bacon |
| orange | orange |
| orange givrée | orange sorbet served in an orange |
| orange pressée | fresh orange juice |
| orangeade | orangeade |

| | |
|---|---|
| oursin | sea urchin |
| pain | bread |
| palette de porc | shoulder of pork |
| palourde | clam |
| pamplemousse | grapefruit |
| panade | bread soup |
| parfait glacé | type of ice cream |
| pastis | anis-flavoured alcoholic drink |
| pâté de canard | duck pâté |
| pâté de foie de volailles | chicken liver pâté |
| pâte feuilletée | puff pastry |
| pâtes | pasta |
| paupiettes de veau | slice of veal rolled and stuffed |
| pêche | peach |
| pêche Melba | peach melba |
| perdreau | young partridge |
| perdrix | partridge |
| pétillant | sparkling |
| petit déjeuner | breakfast |
| petit pain | roll |
| petit pois | pea |
| petit suisse | light white cream cheese |
| petite friture | whitebait |
| petits fours | small fancy pastries |
| pied de porc | pig's trotter |
| pigeon | pigeon |
| pigeonneau | young pigeon |
| pignatelle | small cheese fritter |
| pilaf | rice dish with meat, pilaf |
| pilaf de mouton | rice dish with mutton |
| pintade | guinea fowl |
| piperade | Basque egg dish with tomatoes and pepper |
| pissaladière | Provencal dish similar to pizza |
| pissenlit | dandelion |
| pistache | pistachio |
| plat du jour | dish of the day |
| plateau de fromages | cheese board |
| pochouse | fish casserole with white wine |
| poire | pear |
| poire belle Hélène | pear in chocolate sauce |

| | |
|---|---|
| poireau | leek |
| poisson | fish |
| poivron | pepper |
| pomme | apple |
| pomme bonne femme | baked apple |
| pommes Dauphine | potato fritters |
| pomme de terre | potato |
| pommes de terre à l'anglaise | boiled potatoes |
| pommes de terre en robe de chambre | jacket potatoes |
| pommes de terre en robe des champs | jacket potatoes |
| pommes de terre sautées | sauted potatoes |
| pommes frites | chips, French fries |
| pommes paille | finely cut chips/French fries |
| pommes vapeur | steamed potatoes |
| porc | pork |
| Porto | Port (wine) |
| pot-au-feu | beef and vegetable hot-pot |
| potage | soup |
| potage bilibi | fish and oyster soup |
| potage Crécy | carrot and rice soup |
| potage cressonnière | watercress soup |
| potage Esaü | lentil soup |
| potage parmentier | leek and potato soup |
| potage printanier | vegetable soup |
| potage Saint-Germain | split pea soup |
| potage velouté | creamy soup |
| potée | vegetable and meat hot-pot |
| Pouilly-Fuissé | dry white wine from Burgundy |
| poularde | chicken |
| poule au pot | chicken and vegetable hot-pot |
| poule au riz | chicken with rice |
| poulet à l'estragon | chicken in tarragon sauce |
| poulet basquaise | chicken with ratatouille |
| poulet chasseur | chicken with mushrooms and white wine |
| poulet créole | chicken in white sauce and rice |
| poulet rôti | roast chicken |
| praire | clam |
| prune | plum |

| | |
|---|---|
| **pruneau** | prune |
| **pudding** | spicy bread pudding |
| **purée** | mashed potatoes |
| **purée de marrons** | chestnut purée |
| **purée de pommes de terre** | mashed potatoes |
| **quatre-quarts** | pound cake |
| **quenelle** | meat or fish dumpling |
| **queue de bœuf** | oxtail |
| **quiche lorraine** | quiche |
| **râble de chevreuil** | saddle of venison |
| **raclette** | Swiss dish of melted cheese |
| **ragoût** | stew |
| **raie** | skate *(fish)* |
| **raie au beurre noir** | skate fried in butter |
| **raifort** | horse radish |
| **raisin** | grape |
| **rascasse** | scorpionfish |
| **ratatouille** | dish of courgettes/zucchinis, aubergines/eggplants and tomatoes |
| **ravigote** | dressing with herbs |
| **reblochon** | strong cheese from Savoie |
| **reine-claude** | greengage |
| **rémoulade** | dressing with mustard and herbs |
| **rigotte** | small goat's cheese from Lyons |
| **rillettes** | potted pork or goose meat |
| **ris de veau** | veal sweetbread |
| **rissole** | meat pie |
| **riz** | rice |
| **riz à l'impératrice** | sweet rice dish |
| **riz pilaf** | spicy rice with meat or seafood |
| **rognon** | kidney |
| **rognons au madère** | kidneys in Madeira |
| **roquefort** | blue cheese |
| **rosé** | rosé wine |
| **rôti** | joint |
| **rôti de porc** | roast pork |
| **rouge** | red wine |
| **rouget** | mullet |
| **rouille** | sauce accompanying bouillabaisse |
| **sabayon** | zabaglione *(whipped egg yolk in Marsala wine)* |

| | |
|---|---|
| sablé | shortbread |
| saint-honoré | cream puff cake |
| saint-marcellin | goat's cheese |
| salade | salad, lettuce |
| salade composée | mixed salad |
| salade de tomates | tomato salad |
| salade niçoise | olive, tomato and anchovy salad |
| salade russe | diced vegetable and mayonnaise salad |
| salade verte | green salad |
| salmis | game stew |
| salsifis | oyster plant, salsify |
| sandwich au jambon | ham sandwich |
| sandwich au saucisson | French salami sandwich |
| sanglier | wild boar |
| sardine | sardine |
| sauce aurore | white sauce with tomato puree |
| sauce aux câpres | white sauce with capers |
| sauce béarnaise | thick sauce with eggs and butter |
| sauce blanche | white sauce |
| sauce gribiche | dressing with hard boiled eggs |
| sauce hollandaise | rich sauce served with fish |
| sauce Madère | Madeira sauce |
| sauce matelote | wine sauce |
| sauce Mornay | béchamel sauce with cheese |
| sauce mousseline | hollandaise sauce with cream |
| sauce poulette | sauce with mushrooms and egg yolk |
| sauce ravigote | dressing with shallots and herbs |
| sauce rémoulade | dressing with mustard and herbs |
| sauce suprême | creamy sauce |
| sauce tartare | mayonnaise with herbs and gherkins |
| sauce veloutée | white sauce with egg yolks |
| sauce vinot | wine sauce |
| saucisse | sausage |
| saucisse de Francfort | frankfurter |
| saucisse de Strasbourg | beef sausage |
| saumon | salmon |
| saumon fumé | smoked salmon |
| Sauternes | sweet white wine |
| savarin | crown shaped rum baba |
| sec | dry |

| | |
|---|---|
| seiche | cuttlefish |
| sel | salt |
| service (non) compris | service (not) included |
| service 12% inclus | 12% service charge included |
| servir frais | serve cool |
| sirop | cordial |
| sole | Dover sole |
| soufflé au chocolat | chocolate soufflé |
| soufflé au fromage | cheese soufflé |
| soufflé au Grand Marnier | soufflé with orange liqueur |
| soufflé au jambon | ham soufflé |
| soufflé aux épinards | spinach soufflé |
| soupe | soup |
| soupe à l'ail | garlic soup |
| soupe à l'oignon | onion soup |
| soupe à l'oseille | sorrel soup |
| soupe à la tomate | tomato soup |
| soupe au pistou | thick vegetable soup with basil |
| soupe aux choux | cabbage soup |
| soupe aux moules | mussel soup |
| soupe aux poireaux et pommes de terre | leek and potato soup |
| soupe de poissons | fish soup |
| steak au poivre | pepper steak |
| steak haché | minced meat |
| steak tartare | raw minced meat with a raw egg |
| sucre | sugar |
| tanche | tench *(fish)* |
| tarte | tart, pie |
| tarte aux fraises | strawberry tart/pie |
| tarte aux pommes | apple tart/pie |
| tarte frangipane | almond cream tart/pie |
| tarte Tatin | apple pie |
| tartelette | small tart/pie |
| tartine | slice of bread and butter |
| tendrons de veau | breast of veal |
| terrine | pâté |
| terrine du chef | chef's special pâté |
| tête de veau | calf's head |
| thé | tea |
| thé à la menthe | peppermint tea |

# RESTAURANT

| | |
|---|---|
| **thé au lait** | tea with milk |
| **thé citron** | lemon tea |
| **thon** | tuna fish |
| **tilleul** | lime tea |
| **tomate** | tomato |
| **tomates farcies** | stuffed tomatoes |
| **tome de Savoie** | cheese from Savoy |
| **tournedos** | round fillet of beef |
| **tourte** | pie |
| **tourteau** | kind of crab |
| **tripes** | tripe |
| **tripes à la mode de Caen** | tripe in spicy vegetable sauce |
| **truite à la meunière** | trout fried in butter |
| **truite au bleu** | poached trout |
| **truite aux amandes** | trout fried in butter with almonds |
| **turbot** | turbot |
| **vacherin** | strong cheese from the Jura |
| **vacherin glacé** | ice cream meringue |
| **veau** | veal |
| **velouté de tomate** | cream of tomato soup |
| **vermicelle** | vermicelli *(very fine pasta used in soup)* |
| **verveine** | verbena tea |
| **viande** | meat |
| **vin de pays** | local wine |
| **vin de table** | table wine |
| **vinaigrette** | French dressing |
| **volaille** | poultry |
| **VSOP** | mature brandy |
| **waterzoi de poulet** | chicken with vegetables and cream |
| **yaourt** | yogurt |

66

# SHOPPING

Shops in France are generally open from 8.30am to 7pm, Tuesday to Saturday, and on one Saturday a month there's often an open-air market in the town centre or main street of a district. Here you can buy food, clothes, china etc. at bargain prices.

## USEFUL WORDS AND PHRASES

Refer to the mini-dictionary for items you may want to ask for.

| | | |
|---|---|---|
| **audio equipment** | radio-hifi | *rahdeeo eefee* |
| **baker** | une boulangerie | *boolONjree* |
| **boutique** | une boutique | *booteek* |
| **butcher** | une boucherie | *booshree* |
| **bookshop** | une librairie | *leebrairee* |
| **to buy** | acheter | *ashtay* |
| **cake shop** | une pâtisserie | *patteessree* |
| **cheap** | bon marché | *bON marshay* |
| **chemist** | une pharmacie | *farmassee* |
| **department store** | un grand magasin | *grON magazAN* |
| **fashion** | la mode | *mod* |
| **fishmonger** | une poissonnerie | *pwassonree* |
| **florist** | le fleuriste | *flereest* |
| **grocer** | une épicerie | *aypeessree* |
| **ironmonger** | une quincaillerie | *kANka-yree* |
| **ladies' wear** | des vêtements femmes | *vetmON fam* |
| **menswear** | des vêtements hommes | *vetmON om* |
| **newsagent** | tabac journaux | *tabba joorno* |
| **off-licence,** | vins et liqueurs | *vAN ay leeker* |
| **liquor store** | | |
| **pharmacy** | une pharmacie | *farmassee* |
| **receipt** | un reçu (ticket de caisse) | *ruhsOO (teekay duh kess)* |
| **record shop** | un disquaire | *deeskair* |
| **sale** | les soldes | *solld* |

| | | |
|---|---|---|
| **shoe shop** | un magasin de chaussures | *magazAN duh show-sOOr* |
| **shop** | un magasin | *magazAN* |
| **to go shopping** | faire des courses | *fair day koorss* |
| **souvenir shop** | souvenirs-cadeaux | *soovuhneer kaddo* |
| **special offer** | une offre spéciale | *offr spaysee-al* |
| **to spend** | dépenser | *daypONsay* |
| **stationer** | une papeterie | *pappetree* |
| **supermarket** | un supermarché | *sOOpermarshay* |
| **tailor** | un couturier | *kootOOree-ay* |
| *repairs* | la retoucheuse | *ruhtooshuhz* |
| **take-away** | plats à emporter | *plah ah omportay* |
| **till** | la caisse | *kess* |
| **travel agent** | une agence de voyage | *ajONss duh vwah-yaj* |
| **toyshop** | un magasin de jouets | *magazAN duh joo-ay* |

**I'd like...**
Je voudrais...
*juh voodreh*

**Do you have...?**
Avez-vous...?
*avay voo?*

**How much is...?**
Quel est le prix de...?
*kell eh luh pree duh?*

**Where is the ... department?**
Où se trouve le rayon...?
*oo suh troov luh rayON?*

**Do you have any more of these?**
En avez-vous d'autres?
*ON avay voo doht-r?*

68

**Have you anything cheaper?**
Avez-vous quelque chose de moins cher?
*avay voo kellkuh shose duh mwAN shair?*

**Have you anything larger/smaller?**
Avez-vous quelque chose de plus grand/petit?
*avay voo kellkuh shose duh plOO grON/puhtee?*

**Do you have the next size?**
Avez-vous la taille au-dessus?
*avay voo la tie oh duhsOO?*

**Does it come in other colours?**
L'avez-vous dans d'autres coloris?
*lavay voo dON doht-r koloree?*

**Could you wrap it for me?**
Pouvez-vous me faire un emballage-cadeau?
*poovay voo muh fair AN omballaj kaddo?*

**Can I have a receipt?**
Puis-je avoir un reçu?
*pweej avwahr AN ruhsOO?*

**Can I have a bag please?**
Puis-je avoir une poche?
*pweej avwahr OOn posh?*

**Can I try it on?**
Est-ce que je peux l'essayer?
*esskuh juh puh laissay-yay*

**Where do I pay?**
Où faut-il payer?
*oo fo-teel payay?*

**Can I have a refund?**
Pouvez-vous me rembourser?
*poovay voo muh romboorsay?*

**I'd like to exchange this, it's faulty**
J'aimerais changer cet article. Il ne fonctionne pas bien
*jemmereh shONjay set artee-kl. Eel nuh fONkssi-on pa byAN*

**I'm just looking**
J'aimerais juste regarder
*jemmereh jOOst ruhgarday*

**I'll come back later**
Je reviendrai plus tard
*juh ruhvee-ANdray plOO tar*

---

### *REPLIES YOU MAY BE GIVEN*

**Vous désirez?**
Can I help you?

**Je suis désolé, mais le stock est épuisé**
I'm sorry we are out of stock

**Articles ni repris ni échangés**
Goods will not be exchanged

**Avez-vous de la monnaie?**
Do you have any change?

**Voulez-vous l'essayer?**
Would you like to try it on?

---

### *THINGS YOU'LL SEE OR HEAR*

| | |
|---|---|
| **Agence de voyage** | travel agency |
| **Bon marché** | cheap |
| **Boucher** | butcher |
| **Boucherie** | butcher's |
| **Boulangerie** | bakery |
| **Braderie** | sales |
| **Caddy obligatoire** | please take a trolley |
| **Café** | bar |
| **Centre commercial** | shopping centre |
| **Chausserie** | shoe-shop |
| **Chocolatier** | chocolate shop |
| **Confiserie** | sweet-shop |
| **Entrée gratuite** | admission free |
| **Entrée libre** | admission free |
| **Epicerie** | grocery |
| **Epicerie fine** | delicatessen |
| **Fermeture hebdomadaire** | closed on ... |
| **Fleurs** | flowers |
| **Fleuriste** | flower-shop |
| **Fourreur** | furrier |
| **Frais** | fresh |
| **Fruits et légumes** | greengrocer |
| **Fruits de mer** | seafood |
| **Jouets** | toys |
| **Légumes** | vegetables |
| **Librairie** | book-shop |
| **Location** | rental |
| **Moquette** | carpet |
| **Offre spéciale** | special offer |
| **Panier obligatoire** | please take a basket |
| **Papeterie** | stationery |
| **Parfumerie** | perfume and cosmetics shop |
| **Pâtisserie** | cake-shop |

⟶

| | |
|---|---|
| **Photographe** | camera shop |
| **Poissonnerie** | fishmonger |
| **Primeurs** | greengrocer |
| **Prix** | price |
| **Prix réduit** | reduced price |
| **Prix spécial** | special price |
| **Qualité supérieure** | high quality |
| **Quincaillerie** | ironmonger |
| **Rayon** | department |
| **Réduction** | reduced |
| **Revue** | magazine |
| **Salon de thé** | tea room |
| **Soldes** | sale |
| **Tabac** | tobacco supplies |
| **Une douzaine** | a dozen |
| **Un kilo** | a kilo = 2 pounds |
| **Vêtements enfants** | children's wear |
| **Vêtements femmes** | ladies' wear |
| **Vêtements hommes** | menswear |

# AT THE HAIRDRESSER

## USEFUL WORDS AND PHRASES

| | | |
|---|---|---|
| **appointment** | un rendez-vous | *rONdayvoo* |
| **beard** | la barbe | *barb* |
| **blond** | blond | *blON* |
| **brush** | une brosse | *bross* |
| **comb** | un peigne | *penyuh* |
| **conditioner** | un baume après shampoing | *bohm apreh shompwAN* |
| **curlers** | des rouleaux | *day roolo* |
| **curly** | bouclé | *booklay* |
| **dark** | foncé | *fONssay* |
| **fringe** | la frange | *frONj* |
| **gel** | du gel | *dOO jell* |
| **hair** | les cheveux | *shuhvuh* |
| **haircut** | une coupe | *koop* |
| **hairdresser** (m) | le coiffeur | *kwaffer* |
| **hairdresser** (f) | la coiffeuse | *kwaff-uhz* |
| **hairdryer** | un sèche-cheveux | *sesh shuhvuh* |
| **highlights** | des reflets | *ruhflay* |
| **long** | long | *lON* |
| **moustache** | la moustache | *moostash* |
| **parting** | la raie | *reh* |
| **perm** | une permanente | *pairmanONt* |
| **shampoo** | un shampoing | *shompwAN* |
| **shave** | un rasage | *razzaj* |
| **shaving foam** | de la mousse à raser | *duh la mooss ah razzay* |
| **short** | court | *koor* |
| **styling mousse** | mousse pour les cheveux | *mooss poor lay shuhvuh* |
| **wavy** | ondulé | *ONdOOlay* |

**I'd like to make an appointment**
Je voudrais prendre rendez-vous
*juh voodreh prONdr rONdayvoo*

**Just a trim please**
Je voudrais les faire égaliser
*juh voodreh lay fair aygaleezay*

**Not too much off!**
N'en coupez-pas trop!
*nON koopay pa troh*

**A bit more off here please**
Un petit peu plus court ici
*AN puhtee puh plOO koor ee-see*

**I'd like a cut and blow-dry**
Je voudrais une coupe et un brushing
*juh voodreh OOn koop ay AN brushing*

**I'd like a perm**
Je voudrais une permanente
*juh voodreh OOn pairmanONt*

**I'd like highlights**
Je voudrais des reflets
*juh voodreh day ruhflay*

**I'd like a shampoo and set**
Je voudrais une mise en plis
*juh voodreh OOn meez ON plee*

### *THINGS YOU'LL SEE OR HEAR*

| | |
|---|---|
| **Brushing** | blow dry |
| **Coiffeur** | hairdresser |
| **Coiffeur pour dames** | ladies' hairdresser |
| **Coiffeur pour messieurs** | men's hairdresser |
| **Couleur** | hair-dye |
| **Coupe** | haircut |
| **Derrière** | at the back |
| **Mèches** | streaks |
| **Mini-vague** | demi wave |
| **Mise en plis** | shampoo and set |
| **Raccourcir** | to trim |
| **Salon de coiffure** | hair dressing salon |
| **Sec** | dry |
| **Shampoing** | shampoo |
| **Sur les côtés** | on the sides |

# SPORTS

Wherever you are in France, there's no shortage of sporting facilities whether you want to ski or walk in the mountains, watch soccer or rugby, go fishing, riding, swimming, windsurfing, play golf or tennis. Equipment for all these activities and many more can be hired in most places.

## USEFUL WORDS AND PHRASES

| | | |
|---|---|---|
| **Alps** | les Alpes | *alp* |
| **athletics** | l'athlétisme | *lattlay-teezm* |
| **badminton** | le badminton | *badmeentON* |
| **ball (large)** | un ballon | *ballON* |
| **ball (small)** | une balle | *bal* |
| **bathing suit** | un maillot de bain | *mahyo duh bAN* |
| **beach** | la plage | *plaj* |
| **bicycle** | une bicyclette | *bee-seeklet* |
| | (un vélo) | *(vaylo)* |
| **binding** | les fixations de ski | *feexassi-ON duh skee* |
| **blizzard** | une tempête de neige | *tompet duh nej* |
| **canoe** | un canoë | *kano-ay* |
| **cross-country-skiing** | le ski de fond | *skee duh fON* |
| **current** | le courant | *koorON* |
| **deckchair** | une chaise longue | *shez lONg* |
| **diving board** | un plongeoir | *plONj-warr* |
| **to fish** | pêcher | *peshay* |
| **fishing** | la pêche | *pesh* |
| **fishing rod** | une canne à pêche | *kan ah pesh* |
| **flippers** | des palmes | *palm* |
| **football** | le football (le foot) | *football (foot)* |
| **football match** | un match de football | *mahtch* |
| **golf** | le golf | *golf* |
| **golf course** | un terrain de golf | *terrAN duh golf* |
| **hang-gliding** | le deltaplane | *deltaplan* |

| | | |
|---|---|---|
| **ice-hockey** | le hockey sur glace | *hockey sOOr glass* |
| **ice rink** | une patinoire | *patteenwarr* |
| **jelly-fish** | des méduses | *maidOOz* |
| **lake** | un lac | *lakk* |
| **landing net** | une épuisette | *aypweezet* |
| **lift pass** | un forfait pour | *forfay poor* |
| | remonte-pente | *ruhmONt pONt* |
| **mountaineering** | l'alpinisme | *lalpeeneezm* |
| **parascending** | le parachute | *parashOOt* |
| | ascensionnel | *assOOsee-onnel* |
| **piste, ski trail** | la piste | *peest* |
| **racket** | une raquette | *rakket* |
| **riding** | l'équitation | *layk-eetassiON* |
| **riding helmet** | une bombe | *bombe* |
| **rowing boat** | une barque | *bark* |
| **to run** | courir | *kooreer* |
| **saddle** | une selle | *sell* |
| **sailboard** | une planche à voile | *plONsh ah vwahl* |
| **sailing** | la voile | *vwahl* |
| **sand** | du sable | *sabbl* |
| **sea** | la mer | *mair* |
| **sun bathing** | se faire bronzer | *suh fair brONzay* |
| **to ski** | faire du ski, skier | *fair dOO skee, skee-ay* |
| **ski boots** | des chaussures de ski | *show-sOOr duh skee* |
| **ski lift** | un remonte-pente | *ruhmONt pONt* |
| | (un télésiège) | *(taylaysee-ej)* |
| **skis** | des skis | *skee* |
| **to skate** | faire du patin à glace | *fuir dOO pattAN ah* |
| | (patiner) | *glass (patteenay)* |
| **skates** | des patins à glace | *pattAN ah glass* |
| **sledge** | une luge | *looj* |
| **snorkel** | un tuba | *tOOba* |
| **snow** | la neige | *nej* |
| **stadium** | un stade | *stad* |
| **surfboard** | une planche de surf | *plONsh duh sOOrf* |
| **to swim** | nager | *nahjay* |

| swimming pool | une piscine | *peeseen* |
|---|---|---|
| tennis | le tennis | *tenees* |
| tennis court | un court de tennis | *koor duh* |
| tennis racket | une raquette de | *rakket duh* |
| | tennis | *tenees* |
| tent | une tente | *tONt* |
| tide | la marée | *marray* |
| volleyball | le volleyball (le volley) | *volley* |
| walking | la marche | *marsh* |
| water skis | des skis nautiques | *skee noteek* |
| wave | une vague | *vag* |
| winter sports | les sports d'hiver | *sporr deevair* |
| yacht | un voilier | *vwahlee-ay* |

**How do I get to the beach?**
Quel est le chemin pour la plage?
*kell eh luh shumAN poor la plaj?*

**How deep is the water here?**
Quelle est la profondeur ici?
*kell eh la profONder ee-see?*

**Is there an indoor/outdoor pool here?**
Est-ce qu'il y a une piscine couverte/en plein air ici?
*esskeel-ya OOn peeseen koovert/ON plen air ee-see?*

**Is it safe to swim here?**
Est-ce qu'on peut nager ici sans danger?
*esskON puh nahjay ee-see sON dONjay?*

**Can I fish here?**
Est-ce que la pêche est autorisée ici?
*esskuh la pesh et otoreezay ee-see?*

**Do I need a licence?**
Est-ce que j'ai besoin d'un permis de pêche?
*esskuh jay buhzwAN dAN permee duh pesh?*

**I would like to hire a bike**
Je voudrais louer une bicyclette
*juh voodreh loo-ay OOn bee-seeklet*

**How much does it cost per hour/day?**
Quel est le prix pour une heure/journée?
*kell eh luh pree poor OOn er/joornay?*

**When does the lift start?**
A quelle heure ouvre le remonte-pente?
*ah kell er oovr luh ruhmONt pONt?*

**I would like to take skiing lessons**
Je voudrais prendre des leçons de ski
*juh voodreh prONdr day lessON duh skee*

**Is it very steep?**
Est-ce que la pente est très raide?
*esskuh la pONt eh treh red?*

**Where can I hire...?**
Où est-ce que je peux louer...?
*oo esskuh juh puh looay?*

**How much is a daily/weekly lift pass?**
Quel est le prix d'un forfait journalier/hebdomadaire pour le remonte-pente?
*kell eh luh pree dAN forfay joornal-yay/ebdoma-dair poor luh ruhmont pONt?*

**Where are the nursery slopes?**
Où se trouvent les pistes pour débutants?
*oo suh troov lay peest poor daybOOtON?*

## *THINGS YOU'LL SEE OR HEAR*

| | |
|---|---|
| **Babord** | port side |
| **Barque** | small boat |
| **Bouée** | bouy |
| **Boule** | bowl |
| **Canoë** | canoe |
| **Chasse gardée** | hunting preserve |
| **Courant dangereux** | dangerous current |
| **Equitation** | horse riding |
| **Gymnase** | gymnasium |
| **Location** | for hire |
| **Parachute ascensionnel** | parascending |
| **Patins à glace** | ice skates |
| **Patinoire** | ice rink |
| **Pêche interdite** | no fishing |
| **Pêche sous-marine** | underwater fishing |
| **Pente** | slope |
| **Pétanque** | French bowling game |
| **Piscine** | swimming pool |
| **Piste** | slope |
| **Planche à voile** | sailboard |
| **Planche de surf** | surf board |
| **Plongée sous-marine** | skin diving |
| **Plongeoir** | diving board |
| **Remonte-pente** | ski lift |
| **Stade** | stadium |
| **Terrain de golf** | golf course |
| **Terrain de football** | football pitch |
| **Tribord** | starboard |
| **Vent fort** | strong wind |
| **Voile** | sail |
| **Voilier** | sailing boat |

# POST OFFICE

Post offices in France are open Monday to Friday between 8am and 7pm, and on Saturdays between 8am and noon. Letter boxes are painted yellow. Stamps may be bought in Post offices, Tabac-Journaux and Bar-Tabacs.

## USEFUL WORDS AND PHRASES

| airmail | par avion | *par ah-vee-ON* |
|---|---|---|
| collection | la levée | *luhvay* |
| counter | le guichet | *gheeshay* |
| customs form | un formulaire de douane | *formOOlair duh doo-an* |
| delivery | la distribution | *deestree-bOOssiON* |
| deposit | un versement | *versuhmON* |
| form | un formulaire | *formOOlair* |
| letter | une lettre | *lettr* |
| letter box | la boîte à lettres | *bwat ah lettr* |
| mail | le courrier | *kooree-ay* |
| main post office | la poste principale | *post prANsee-pal* |
| money order | un mandat | *mONda* |
| package | un paquet | *pakkay* |
| parcel | un colis | *kolee* |
| post, mail | la poste | *post* |
| postage rates | les tarifs postaux | *tareef postoh* |
| postal order | un mandat | *mONda* |
| postcard | une carte postale | *kart postal* |
| postcode | le code postal | *kod postal* |
| poste-restante | la poste restante | *post restONt* |
| postman | le facteur | *fakter* |
| post office | la poste | *posst* |
| registered letter | une lettre recommandée | *lettr ruh-kommONday* |
| savings | l'épargne | *ayparn* |
| stamp | un timbre | *tANbr* |

| **surface mail** | par voie de terre | *par vwah duh ter* |
| **telegram** | un télégramme | *taylaygram* |
| **telephone** | le téléphone | *taylayfon* |
| **telephone kiosk** | la cabine téléphonique | *kabeen taylayfoneek* |
| **withdrawal** | un retrait | *ruhtreh* |

**How much is a letter/postcard to...?**
Quel est le tarif pour une lettre/carte postale pour...?
*kell eh luh tareef poor OOn lettr/kart postal poor?*

**I would like three ... franc stamps**
Je voudrais trois timbres à ... francs
*juh voodreh trwah tANbr ah ... frON*

**I want to register this letter**
Je voudrais envoyer cette lettre en recommandé
*juh voodreh ONvwah-yay set lettr ON ruhkommONday*

**I want to send this parcel to...**
Je voudrais envoyer ce colis à...
*juh voodreh ONvwah-yay suh kolee ah*

**How long does the post/mail to ... take?**
Combien de temp mettent les lettres pour...?
*kombyAN duh tON met lay lettr poor?*

**Where can I post/mail this?**
Où est-ce que je peux poster ceci?
*oo esskuh juh puh postay suhsee?*

**I want to make an international call**
Je veux téléphoner à l'étranger
*juh vuh taylayfonay ah laytrONjay*

**Is there any mail for me?**
Y a-t-il du courrier pour moi?
*ee ahteel dOO kooree-ay poor mwah?*

**I'd like to send a telegram**
Je voudrais envoyer un télégramme
*juh voodreh ONvwah-yay AN taylaygram*

**This is to go airmail**
Cela doit être expédié par avion
*suhla dwah etr expaydee-ay par ah-vee-ON*

## *THINGS YOU'LL SEE OR HEAR*

| | |
|---|---|
| **Accusé de réception** | acknowledgement of receipt |
| **Aérogramme** | aerogram |
| **Adresse** | address |
| **Affranchir** | to stamp |
| **Affranchissement** | postage |
| **Autres destinations** | other destinations |
| **Bureau de poste** | post office |
| **Carnet de timbres** | book of stamps |
| **Carte postale** | postcard |
| **Colis** | parcel |
| **Courrier recommandé** | registered mail |
| **Destinataire** | addressee |
| **Expéditeur** | sender |
| **Fermé** | closed |
| **Guichet** | counter |
| **Heures d'ouverture** | hours of opening |
| **Lettre** | letter |
| **Mandat** | postal order |
| **Ne pas affranchir** | free post |
| **Ouvert** | open |
| **Paquet** | package |
| **Par avion** | air mail |
| **P et T (postes et télécommunications)** | post office (with telephone) |
| **Prochaine levée** | next collection |
| **Retrait** | withdrawal |
| **Télégramme** | telegram |
| **Timbre** | stamp |
| **Versement** | deposit |
| **Ville** | town |

# TELEPHONE

Telephone boxes in France are square stainless steel kiosks. They work with coins (50 centimes, 1 franc and 5 francs). If your call is not answered, the coins are retrieved by putting the receiver down. International calls can be made from all of them. In Paris you'll find the "taxiphone" in some cafés; this works with a "jeton" instead of coins, but is now being replaced by the same system found in telephone boxes. To telephone the UK (or USA) from France, dial 19 and wait for the musical signal, then dial 44 (or 1 for USA) followed by the area code and the number you want. (Note, do **not** dial the 0 which prefixes all area code numbers in the UK). The tones you'll hear differ slightly from those heard on our phones:

Dialling tone: same as in UK or USA
Ringing: repeated long tone
Engaged: same as in UK or USA
Unobtainable: voice says "Il n'y a pas d'abonné au numéro que vous avez demandé, veuillez consulter l'annuaire ou l'opératrice".

Since October 1985 all French telephone numbers have 8 figures. They are read out in pairs of numbers, i.e. 45826432 is said "quarante cinq, quatre-vingt deux, soixante quatre, trente deux" (forty five, eighty two, sixty four, thirty two).

## USEFUL WORDS AND PHRASES

| | | |
|---|---|---|
| **call** | un appel | *appel* |
| **to call** | appeler | *applay* |
| **code** | l'indicatif | *lANdeekateef* |
| **to dial** | composer un numéro | *kompozay AN nOOmero* |
| **dialling tone** | la tonalité | *tonaleetay* |
| **emergency** | urgence | *OOrjONss* |
| **enquiries** | les renseignements | *rONsen-yuhmON* |
| **extension** | la poste | *posst* |
| **international call** | communication à l'étranger | *kommOOneeka-siON ah laytrONjay* |

| | | |
|---|---|---|
| **number** | le numéro | *nOOmero* |
| **operator** | l'opératrice | *lopay-ratreess* |
| **pay-phone** | téléphone public | *taylayfon pOObleek* |
| **push-button phone** | téléphone à touches | *taylayfon ah toosh* |
| **receiver** | l'écouteur | *laikooter* |
| **reverse charge call** | une communication en P.C.V. | *kommOOneeka-siON ON pay say vay* |
| **ringing tone** | la sonnerie | *sonneree* |
| **telephone** | le téléphone | *taylayfon* |
| **telephone box** | une cabine téléphonique | *kabeen taylay-foneek* |
| **telephone directory** | l'annuaire | *lannOO-air* |
| **wrong number** | un faux numéro | *foh nOOmero* |

**Where is the nearest phone box?**
Où se trouve la cabine téléphonique la plus proche?
*oo suh troov la kabeen taylayfoneek la plOO prosh?*

**Is there a telephone directory?**
Y a-t-il un annuaire?
*ee-ateel AN annOOair?*

**I would like the directory for...**
Je voudrais l'annuaire de...
*juh voodreh lannOO-air duh*

**Can I call abroad from here?**
Est-ce que je peux appeler l'étranger d'ici?
*esskuh juh puh applay laytrONjay dee-see?*

**How much is a call to...?**
Quel est le prix d'une communication pour...?
*kell eh luh pree dOOn kommOOneekassiON poor?*

**We've got a crossed line**
La ligne cst encombrée
*la leen et ONkombray*

**I would like to reverse the charges**
Je voudrais téléphoner en P.C.V.
*juh voodreh taylayfonay ON pay say vay*

**I would like a number in...**
Je voudrais un numéro à/en...
*juh voodreh AN nOOmero ah/ON*

**Hello, this is ... speaking**
Allô! ... à l'appareil
*allo! ... ah lapparay*

**Is that...?**
Est-ce que je suis chez...?
*esskuh juh swee shay?*

**Speaking** (man/woman)
Lui-même/elle-même
*lwee mem/el mem*

**I would like to speak to...**
Je voudrais parler à...
*juh voodreh parlay ah*

**Extension ... please**
Le poste ..., s'il vous plaît
*luh posst ... seel voo pleh*

**Please tell him ... called**
Pouvez-vous lui dire que ... a téléphoné?
*poovay voo lwee deer kuh ... ah taylayfonay?*

**Ask him to call me back please**
Pouvez-vous lui demander de me rappeler?
*poovay voo lwee duhmONday duh muh rapplay?*

**My number is...**
Mon numéro est le...
*mON nOOmero eh luh...*

**Do you know where he is?**
Savez-vous où je peux le contacter?
*sahvay voo oo juh puh luh kontaktay?*

**When will he be back?**
Savez-vous quand il sera de retour?
*sahvay voo kON eel suhra duh ruhtoor?*

**Could you leave him a message?**
Pouvez-vous lui laisser un message?
*poovay voo lwee lessay AN muhssaj?*

**I'll ring back later**
Je rappellerai plus tard
*juh rappelray plOO tar*

**Sorry, I've got the wrong number**
Excusez-moi, je me suis trompé de numéro
*exkOOzay mwah, juh muh swee trompay duh nOOmero*

**The phone is out of order**
Le téléphone est en dérangement
*luh taylayfon et ON dayrONjmON*

**Please connect me with this number**
Pouvez-vous m'appeler ce numéro, s'il vous plaît?
*poovay voo mapplay suh nOOmero, seel voo pleh?*

## *THINGS YOU'LL SEE OR HEAR*

**A quel numéro pouvons-nous vous joindre?**
At what number can we contact you?

**A qui désirez-vous parler?**
Who would you like to speak to?

**Elle-même**
Speaking *(when a woman)*

**Il sera de retour à...**
He'll be back at...

**J'écoute**
Speaking

**La ligne est encombrée**
The line is busy

**Lui-même**
Speaking *(when a man)*

**Ne quittez pas**
Hold the line please

**Ne raccrochez pas**
Hang on, please

**Pouvez-vous rappeler plus tard?**
Could you phone later?

**Quel numéro demandez-vous?**
Which number do you want?

$\longrightarrow$

89

**Qui est à l'appareil?**
Who is speaking?

**Voulez-vous rappeler plus tard?**
Would you like to phone later?

| | |
|---|---|
| **Allô?** | hello? |
| **Appareil** | (the) telephone |
| **Botin** | directory |
| **Cabine téléphonique** | telephone box |
| **Combiné** | receiver |
| **Communication** | call |
| **Communication interurbaine** | long distance call |
| **Décrocher** | to pick up |
| **En dérangement** | out of order |
| **Faux numéro** | wrong number |
| **Indicatif** | code |
| **Introduire** | to insert |
| **Occupé** | engaged |
| **Pièce** | coin |
| **Pompiers** | Fire Brigade |
| **Pulsation** | unit |
| **Réclamations** | faults service |
| **Renseignements** | enquiries |
| **Reposer** | to put down |
| **Sonnerie** | ringing |
| **Tonalité** | tone |

# HEALTH

Under the EEC Social Security regulations visitors from the UK qualify for treatment on the same basis as the French themselves. You must complete the form CM1 (at your own Social Security office) a month at least before travelling. You then get a certificate (E111) for use if you need treatment, plus an explanatory leaflet.

If you are suddenly taken ill and need medicine, a Chemist's is called a "Pharmacie". At night and on Sundays there is "la pharmacie de garde" (duty chemist). You can find its address in the local newspaper, in the window of any chemist or through the local "commissariat de police". If you have a prescription from your doctor at home, it will have to be rewritten by a French doctor. Some chemists specialise in English medicine and if you have not brought (or if they don't stock) the remedy you require they can always recommend a substitute.

## USEFUL WORDS AND PHRASES

| | | |
|---|---|---|
| **accident** | un accident | *akseedON* |
| **ambulance** | une ambulance | *ombOOlONss* |
| **anaemic** | anémique | *annaymeek* |
| **appendicitis** | une appendicite | *appONdee-seet* |
| **appendix** | l'appendice | *lappONdeess* |
| **aspirin** | de l'aspirine | *duh laspeereen* |
| **asthma** | l'asthme | *laz-m* |
| **backache** | mal au dos | *mal oh doh* |
| **bandage** | un pansement | *pONssmON* |
| **bite** | une morsure | *morsOOr* |
| **(of insect)** | (une piqûre) | *(peekOOr)* |
| **bladder** | la vessie | *vessee* |
| **blister** | une ampoule | *ompool* |
| **blood** | du sang | *sON* |
| **blood donor** | un donneur de sang | *donner duh sON* |
| **brace** | un appareil | *apparray* |
| **burn** | une brûlure | *brOOlOOr* |

91

| | | |
|---|---|---|
| **cancer** | le cancer | *kONsair* |
| **catarrh** | le rhume | *rOOm* |
| **chemist** | la pharmacie | *farmassee* |
| **chest** | la poitrine | *pwattreen* |
| **chicken pox** | la varicelle | *varree-sel* |
| **cold** | un rhume | *rOOm* |
| **concussion** | une commotion cérébrale | *kommossiON sayraybral* |
| **constipation** | la constipation | *konstee-passiON* |
| **contact lenses** | des verres de contact (lentilles) | *vair duh kONtakt (lONtee)* |
| **corn** | un cor | *kor* |
| **cotton wool** | du coton hydrophile | *dOO kotON eedrofeel* |
| **cough** | la toux | *too* |
| **cut** | une coupure | *koopOOr* |
| **dentist** | le dentiste | *dONteest* |
| **diabetes** | du diabète | *dOO dee-abet* |
| **diarrhoea** | la diarrhée | *dee-array* |
| **dizzy** | le vertige | *verrteej* |
| **doctor** | le docteur | *dokter* |
| **earache** | mal à l'oreille | *mal ah loray* |
| **fever** | la fièvre | *fee-evr* |
| **filling** | un plombage | *plombaj* |
| **first aid** | premiers soins | *pruhmee-ay swAN* |
| **flu** | la grippe | *greep* |
| **fracture** | une fracture | *fraktOOr* |
| **German measles** | la rubéole | *rOObay-ol* |
| **glasses** | des lunettes | *lOO-net* |
| **haemorrhage** | une hémoragie | *aymorajee* |
| **hayfever** | le rhume des foins | *rOOm day fwAN* |
| **headache** | des maux de tête | *mo duh tet* |
| **heart** | le cœur | *ker* |
| **heart attack** | une crise cardiaque | *kreez kardee-ak* |
| **hospital** | l'hôpital | *lopeetahl* |
| **ill** | malade | *malad* |
| **indigestion** | une indigestion | *ANdeejestiON* |
| **injection** | une piqûre | *peekOOr* |

| | | |
|---|---|---|
| **itch** | des démangeaisons | *daymONjezON* |
| **kidney** | les reins | *rAN* |
| **laxative** | un laxatif | *laxateef* |
| **lung** | les poumons | *poomON* |
| **lump** | une grosseur | *grosser* |
| **measles** | la rougeole | *roojol* |
| **migraine** | la migraine | *meegren* |
| **mumps** | les oreillons | *oray-yON* |
| **nausea** | la nausée | *nozay* |
| **nurse** | l'infirmière | *lANfeermee-yer* |
| **operation** | une opération | *opayrassiON* |
| **optician** | un opticien | *optee-seeAN* |
| **pain** | une douleur | *dooler* |
| **penicillin** | la péniciline | *paynee-seeleen* |
| **pneumonia** | une pneumonie | *p-nuhmonee* |
| **pregnant** | enceinte | *ONsANt* |
| **prescription** | une ordonnance | *ordonnONss* |
| **rheumatism** | des rhumatismes | *rOOmatteesm* |
| **scald** | une brûlure | *brOOlOOr* |
| **scratch** | une égratignure | *aygratteen-yOOr* |
| **smallpox** | la variole | *varree-ol* |
| **sore throat** | mal à la gorge | *mal ah la gorj* |
| **splinter** | une écharde | *aishard* |
| **sprain** | une entorse | *ONtorss* |
| **sticking plaster** | un pansement | *pONssmON* |
| **sting** | une piqûre | *peekOOr* |
| **stomach** | l'estomac | *lestoma* |
| **sun stroke** | une insolation | *ANsolassiON* |
| **temperature** | la température | *tompayratOOr* |
| **throat** | la gorge | *gorj* |
| **tonsils** | les amygdales | *ammeedal* |
| **tooth** | la dent | *dON* |
| **toothache** | mal aux dents | *mal oh dON* |
| **travel sickness** | mal des transports | *mal day trONspor* |
| **ulcer** | un ulcère | *OOl-sair* |
| **vaccination** | un vaccin | *vakksAN* |

| **verruca** | une verrue plantaire | *vayrOO plON-tair* |
| **to vomit** | vomir | *vomeer* |
| **whooping cough** | la coqueluche | *koklOOsh* |
| **wisdom tooth** | une dent de sagesse | *dON duh sajess* |

**I have a pain in...**
J'ai mal au...
*jay mal oh*

**I do not feel well**
Je ne me sens pas bien
*juh nuh muh sON pa byAN*

**I feel faint**
Je vais m'évanouir
*juh veh mayvanoo-eer*

**I feel sick**
J'ai envie de vomir
*jay ONvee duh vomeer*

**I feel dizzy**
J'ai la tête qui tourne
*jay la tet kee toorn*

**It hurts here**
J'ai mal ici
*jay mal ee-see*

**It's a sharp pain**
C'est une douleur aigüe
*set OOn dooler ay-gOO*

**It's a dull pain**
C'est une douleur sourde
*set OOn dooler soord*

**It hurts all the time**
La douleur est constante
*la dooler eh kONstONt*

**It only hurts now and then**
C'est douloureux de temps en temps
*seh doolooruh duh tON zON tON*

**It hurts when you touch it**
C'est douloureux seulement au toucher
*seh doolooruh suhlmON oh tooshay*

**It hurts more at night**
C'est douloureux surtout la nuit
*seh doolooruh sOOrtoo la nwee*

**It stings**
Ça pique
*sa peek*

**It aches**
Ça fait mal
*sa feh mal*

**I need a prescription for...**
J'ai besoin d'une ordonnance pour...
*jay buhzwAN dOOn ordonnONss poor*

**I normally take...**
Je prends habituellement...
*juh prON abeetOO-elmON*

**I'm allergic to...**
Je suis allergique à...
*juh sweez allerjeek ah*

**Have you got anything for...?**
Avez-vous quelque chose contre...?
*avay voo kellkuh shose kONtr?*

**Do I need a prescription for...?**
Me faut-il une ordonnance pour...?
*muh fo-teel OOn ordonnONss poor?*

---

### REPLIES YOU MAY BE GIVEN

**Prendre ... comprimés à la fois**
Take ... tablets at a time

**Prendre ... comprimés ... fois par jour**
Take ... tablets ... times a day

**Avec de l'eau/mâchez-les**
With water/chew them

**A prendre au coucher**
To be taken at bedtime

**Le matin à jeun**
First thing in the morning

**Que prenez-vous habituellement?**
What do you normally take?

**Je pense que vous devriez voir un docteur**
I think you should see a doctor

**Il vous faut une ordonnance pour ça**
You need a prescription for that

**On ne trouve pas cela ici**
You cannot get that here

---

### *THINGS YOU'LL SEE OR HEAR*

| | |
|---|---|
| **Ambulance** | ambulance |
| **Anesthésie locale** | local anesthetic |
| **Anesthésie générale** | general anesthetic |
| **Cabinet dentaire** | dentist's surgery |
| **Cabinet médical** | doctor's surgery |
| **Clinique** | clinic |
| **Dentiste** | dentist |
| **Dermatologue** | dermatologist |
| **Docteur** | doctor |
| **Généraliste** | GP |
| **Gynécologue** | gynaecologist |
| **Hôpital** | hospital |
| **Médecin** | doctor |
| **Oto-rhino-laryngologiste** | ear, nose and throat specialist |
| **Pédiatre** | paediatrician |
| **Pharmacie** | chemist (shop) |
| **Pharmacie de service** | duty chemist |
| **Pharmacien** | chemist |
| **Service** | ward |
| **Service d'urgence** | emergency ward |
| **S.O.S. Médecin** | 24h emergency medical service found in large towns |
| **Spécialiste** | specialist |

# CONVERSION TABLES

## DISTANCES

Distances are marked in kilometres. To convert kilometres to miles, divide the km. by 8 and multiply by 5 (one km. being five-eighths of a mile). Convert miles to km. by dividing the miles by 5 and multiplying by 8. A mile is 1609m. (1.609km.).

| km. | miles or km. | miles |
|---|---|---|
| 1.61 | **1** | 0.62 |
| 3.22 | **2** | 1.24 |
| 4.83 | **3** | 1.86 |
| 6.44 | **4** | 2.48 |
| 8.05 | **5** | 3.11 |
| 9.66 | **6** | 3.73 |
| 11.27 | **7** | 4.35 |
| 12.88 | **8** | 4.97 |
| 14.49 | **9** | 5.59 |
| 16.10 | **10** | 6.21 |
| 32.20 | **20** | 12.43 |
| 48.28 | **30** | 18.64 |
| 64.37 | **40** | 24.85 |
| 80.47 | **50** | 31.07 |
| 160.93 | **100** | 62.14 |
| 321.90 | **200** | 124.30 |
| 804.70 | **500** | 310.70 |
| 1609.34 | **1000** | 621.37 |

Other units of length:

| | |
|---|---|
| 1 centimetre = 0.39 in. | 1 inch = 25.4 millimetres |
| 1 metre = 39.37 in. | 1 foot = 0.30 metre (30 cm.) |
| 10 metres = 32.81 ft. | 1 yard = 0.91 metre |

## WEIGHTS

The unit you will come into most contact with is the kilogram (kilo), equivalent to 2 lb 3 oz. To convert kg. to lbs., multiply by 2 and add one-tenth of the result (thus, 6 kg x 2 = 12 + 1.2, or 13.2 lbs). One ounce is about 28 grams, and 1 lb is 454 g. One UK hundredweight is almost 51 kg; one USA cwt is 45 kg. One UK ton is 1016 kg (USA ton = 907 kg).

| grams | ounces | | ounces | grams |
|---|---|---|---|---|
| 50 | 1.76 | | 1 | 28.3 |
| 100 | 3.53 | | 2 | 56.7 |
| 250 | 8.81 | | 4 | 113.4 |
| 500 | 17.63 | | 8 | 226.8 |

| kg. | lbs. or kg. | lbs. |
|---|---|---|
| 0.45 | 1 | 2.20 |
| 0.91 | 2 | 4.41 |
| 1.36 | 3 | 6.61 |
| 1.81 | 4 | 8.82 |
| 2.27 | 5 | 11.02 |
| 2.72 | 6 | 13.23 |
| 3.17 | 7 | 15.43 |
| 3.63 | 8 | 17.64 |
| 4.08 | 9 | 19.84 |
| 4.53 | 10 | 22.04 |
| 9.07 | 20 | 44.09 |
| 11.34 | 25 | 55.11 |
| 22.68 | 50 | 110.23 |
| 45.36 | 100 | 220.46 |

## LIQUIDS

Motorists from the UK will be used to seeing petrol priced per litre (and may even know that one litre is about $1\frac{3}{4}$ pints). One 'imperial' gallon is roughly $4\frac{1}{2}$ litres, but USA drivers must remember that the American gallon is only 3.8 litres (1 litre = 1.06 US quart). In the following table, imperial gallons are used:

| litres | gals. or 1. | gals. |
|--------|-------------|-------|
| 4.54   | 1           | 0.22  |
| 9.10   | 2           | 0.44  |
| 13.64  | 3           | 0.66  |
| 18.18  | 4           | 0.88  |
| 22.73  | 5           | 1.10  |
| 27.27  | 6           | 1.32  |
| 31.82  | 7           | 1.54  |
| 36.37  | 8           | 1.76  |
| 40.91  | 9           | 1.98  |
| 45.46  | 10          | 2.20  |
| 90.92  | 20          | 4.40  |
| 136.38 | 30          | 6.60  |
| 181.84 | 40          | 8.80  |
| 227.30 | 50          | 11.00 |

## TYRE PRESSURES

| lb/sq.in. | 15  | 18  | 20  | 22  | 24  |
|-----------|-----|-----|-----|-----|-----|
| kg/sq.cm. | 1.1 | 1.3 | 1.4 | 1.5 | 1.7 |

| lb/sq.in. | 26  | 28  | 30  | 33  | 35  |
|-----------|-----|-----|-----|-----|-----|
| kg/sq.cm. | 1.8 | 2.0 | 2.1 | 2.3 | 2.5 |

## AREA

The average tourist isn't all that likely to need metric area conversions, but with more 'holiday home' plots being bought overseas nowadays it might be useful to know that 1 square metre = 10.8 square feet, and that the main unit of land area measurement is a hectare (which is 2½ acres). The hectare is 10,000 sq.m. - for convenience, visualise something roughly 100 metres or yards square. To convert hectares to acres, divide by 2 and multiply by 5 (and vice-versa).

| hectares | acres *or* ha. | acres |
|---|---|---|
| 0.4 | **1** | 2.5 |
| 2.0 | **5** | 12.4 |
| 4.1 | **10** | 24.7 |
| 20.2 | **50** | 123.6 |
| 40.5 | **100** | 247.1 |

## TEMPERATURE

To convert centigrade or Celsius degrees into Fahrenheit, the accurate method is to multiply the °C figure by 1.8 and add 32. Similarly, to convert °F to °C, subtract 32 from the °F figure and divide by 1.8. This will give you a truly accurate conversion, but takes a little time in mental arithmetic! See the table below. If all you want is some idea of how hot it is forecast to be in the sun, simply double the °C figure and add 30; the °F result will be overstated by a degree or two when the answer is in the 60-80°F range, while 90°F should be 86°F.

| °C | °F | | °C | °F | |
|---|---|---|---|---|---|
| -10 | 14 | | 25 | 77 | |
| 0 | 32 | | 30 | 86 | |
| 5 | 41 | | 36.9 | 98.4 | body temperature |
| 10 | 50 | | 40 | 104 | |
| 20 | 68 | | 100 | 212 | boiling point |

## CLOTHING SIZES

Slight variations in sizes, let alone European equivalents of UK/USA sizes, will be found everywhere so be sure to check before you buy. The following tables are approximate:

*Women's dresses and suits*

| UK | 10 | 12 | 14 | 16 | 18 | 20 |
|---|---|---|---|---|---|---|
| **Europe** | **36** | **38** | **40** | **42** | **44** | **46** |
| USA | 8 | 10 | 12 | 14 | 16 | 18 |

*Men's suits and coats*

| UK/USA | 36 | 38 | 40 | 42 | 44 | 46 |
|---|---|---|---|---|---|---|
| **Europe** | **46** | **48** | **50** | **52** | **54** | **56** |

*Women's shoes*

| UK | 4 | 5 | 6 | 7 | 8 |
|---|---|---|---|---|---|
| **Europe** | **37** | **38** | **39** | **41** | **42** |
| USA | $5\frac{1}{2}$ | $6\frac{1}{2}$ | $7\frac{1}{2}$ | $8\frac{1}{2}$ | $9\frac{1}{2}$ |

*Men's shoes*

| UK/USA | 7 | 8 | 9 | 10 | 11 |
|---|---|---|---|---|---|
| **Europe** | **41** | **42** | **43** | **44** | **45** |

*Men's shirts*

| UK/USA | 14 | $14\frac{1}{2}$ | 15 | $15\frac{1}{2}$ | 16 | $16\frac{1}{2}$ | 17 |
|---|---|---|---|---|---|---|---|
| **Europe** | **36** | **37** | **38** | **39** | **41** | **42** | **43** |

*Women's sweaters*

| UK/USA | 32 | 34 | 36 | 38 | 40 |
|---|---|---|---|---|---|
| **Europe** | **36** | **38** | **40** | **42** | **44** |

*Waist and chest measurements*

| Inches | 28 | 30 | 32 | 34 | 36 | 38 | 40 | 42 | 44 | 46 |
|---|---|---|---|---|---|---|---|---|---|---|
| Cms | 71 | 76 | 80 | 87 | 91 | 97 | 102 | 107 | 112 | 117 |

# MINI-DICTIONARY

accelerator l'accélérateur
accident l'accident
accommodation l'hébergement
ache la douleur
adaptor *(electrical)* la prise
  multiple
addresss l'adresse
adhesive l'adhésif
after après
after-shave l'après-rasage
again de nouveau
against contre
air l'air
air freshener le désodorisant
air hostess l'hôtesse de l'air
air-conditioning la climatisation
aircraft l'avion
airline la compagnie aérienne
airport l'aéroport
alcohol l'alcool
Algeria l'Algérie
Algerian algérien
all tout
  all the streets toutes les rues
almost presque
alone seul
Alps les Alpes
already déjà
always toujours
am: I am je suis
ambulance l'ambulance
America l'Amérique
American américain
and et
Andorra Andorre
ankle la cheville
anorak l'anorak
another un autre
anti-freeze l'antigel

antique shop le magasin
  d'antiquités
antiseptic l'antiseptique
aperitif l'apéritif
appendicitis l'appendicite
appetite l'appétit
apple la pomme
application form le formulaire de
  demande
appointment le rendez-vous
apricot l'abricot
are: you are vous êtes
  *(singular familiar)* tu es
  we are nous sommes
  they are ils/elles sont
arm le bras
art l'art
art gallery le musée d'art
artist l'artiste
ashtray le cendrier
asleep endormi
  he's asleep il dort
aspirin l'aspirine
at: at the post office à la poste
  at night la nuit
  at 3 o'clock à 3 heures
attractive attirant
aunt la tante
Australia l'Australie
Australian australien
Austria l'Autriche
Austrian autrichien
automatic automatique
away: is it far away? est-ce que
  c'est loin?
  go away! allez-vous en!
awful affreux
axe la hache
axle l'essieu

**baby** le bébé
**back** *(not front)* l'arrière
  *(body)* le dos
**bacon** le bacon
  **bacon and eggs** des œufs au bacon
**bad** mauvais
**bait** l'appât
**bake** cuire
**baker** le boulanger
**balcony** le balcon
**ball** *(football)* le ballon
  *(tennis)* la balle
  *(dance)* le bal
**ball-point pen** le stylo-bille
**banana** la banane
**band** *(musicians)* le groupe
**bandage** le pansement
**bank** la banque
**banknote** le billet
**bar** le bar
  **bar of chocolate** la tablette de chocolat
**barbecue** le barbecue
**barber** le coiffeur
**bargain** une affaire
**basement** le sous-sol
**basin** la cuvette
  *(sink)* le lavabo
**basket** le panier
**bath** la bain
  **to have a bath** prendre un bain
**bath salts** les sels de bain
**bathing hat** une charlotte
**bathroom** la salle de bain
**battery** *(car)* la batterie
  *(torch)* la pile
**beach** la plage

**beans** les haricots
**beard** la barbe
**because** parce que
**bed** le lit
**bed linen** les draps
**bedroom** la chambre
**beef** le bœuf
**beer** la bière
**before** avant
**beginner** le débutant
**behind** derrière
**beige** beige
**Belgian** belge
**Belgium** la Belgique
**bell** *(church)* la cloche
  *(door)* la sonnette
**belt** la ceinture
**beside** à côté de
**better** mieux
**between** entre
**bicycle** la bicyclette
**big** grand
**bikini** le bikini
**bill** l'addition
**bin liner** le sac poubelle
**binding** *(ski)* la fixation
**bird** l'oiseau
**birthday** l'anniversaire
  **happy birthday!** joyeux anniversaire!
**birthday card** la carte d'anniversaire
**biscuit** le biscuit
**bite** *(verb)* mordre
  *(noun)* la morsure
**bitter** amer
**black** noir
**blackberry** la mûre
**blackcurrant** le cassis
**blanket** la couverture
**bleach** *(verb)* décolorer
  *(noun)* l'eau de Javel (R)

**blind** *(cannot see)* aveugle
  *(window)* le store
**blister** l'ampoule
**blood** le sang
**blouse** le chemisier
**blue** bleu
**boat** le bateau
  *(smaller)* la barque
**body** le corps
**boil** bouillir
**bolt** *(verb)* verrouiller
  *(noun: on door)* le verrou
**bone** l'os
  *(fish)* l'arête
**bonnet** *(car)* le capot
**book** *(noun)* le livre
  *(verb)* réserver
**booking office** *(railway station)*
  le bureau des réservations
  *(theatre etc)* le bureau de
  location des places
**bookshop** la librairie
**boot** *(car)* le coffre
  *(footwear)* la botte
**border** la frontière
**boring** ennuyeux
**born: I was born in ...** je suis
  né en ...
**both** les deux
  **both of them** tous les deux
  **both of us** nous deux
  **both ... and ...** ... et ... à la
  fois
**bottle** la bouteille
**bottle-opener** le décapsuleur
**bottom** le fond
**bowl** le bol
**box** la boîte
**boy** le garçon
**boyfriend** le petit ami
**bra** le soutien-gorge
**bracelet** le bracelet

**braces** les bretelles
**brake** *(noun)* le frein
  *(verb)* freiner
**brandy** le cognac
**bread** le pain
**breakdown** *(car)* la panne
  *(nervous)* la dépression
**breakfast** le petit déjeuner
**breathe** respirer
  **I can't breathe** j'étouffe
**bridge** le pont
**briefcase** l'attaché-case
**Brittany** la Bretagne
**brochure** la brochure
**broken** cassé
  **broken leg** la jambe
  cassée
**brooch** la broche
**brother** le frère
**brown** marron
**bruise** le bleu
**brush** *(noun)* la brosse
  *(paint)* le pinceau
  *(verb)* brosser
**bucket** le seau
**building** le bâtiment
**bumper** les pare-chocs
**burn** *(verb)* brûler
  *(noun)* la brûlure
**bus** le bus
**bus station** la gare d'autobus
**business** les affaires
  **it's none of your business** cela
  ne vous regarde pas
**busker** le musicien des rues
**busy** *(occupied)* occupé
  *(street)* animé
**but** mais
**butcher** le boucher
**butter** le beurre
**button** le bouton
**buy** acheter

**by: by the window** près de la
fenêtre
 **by Friday** d'ici vendredi
 **by myself** tout seul

**cabbage** le chou
**cable car** le téléphérique
**café** le café
**cagoule** le K-way (R)
**cake** le gâteau
**cake shop** la pâtisserie
**calculator** la calculette
**camera** l'appareil-photo
**campsite** le terrain de camping
**camshaft** l'arbre à cames
**can** *(able)* pouvoir
 *(tin)* la boîte de conserve
 **can I have ...?** puis-je avoir ...?
**Canada** le Canada
**Canadian** canadien
**canal** le canal
**cancer** le cancer
**candle** la bougie
**canoe** le canoë
**cap** la casquette
**car** la voiture
**caravan** la caravane
**carburettor** le carburateur
**card** la carte
**cardigan** le gilet
**careful** prudent
 **careful!** attention!
 **be careful!** soyez prudent!
**carpet** le tapis
**carriage** *(train)* la voiture
**carrot** la carotte
**carry-cot** le porte-bébé
**case** la valise
**cash** l'argent

*(change)* la monnaie
 **to pay cash** payer en liquide
**cassette** la cassette
**cassette player** le lecteur de
cassettes
**castle** le château
**cat** le chat
**cathedral** la cathédrale
**cauliflower** le chou-fleur
**cave** la grotte
**cemetery** le cimetière
**certificate** le certificat
**chair** la chaise
**chamber music** la musique de
chambre
**chambermaid** la femme de
chambre
**change** *(money)* la monnaie
 *(clothes)* les habits de rechange
 *(verb)* changer
**Channel** la Manche
**Channel Islands** les îles
Anglo-Normandes
**cheap** pas cher
**cheers!** santé!
**cheese** le fromage
**chemist** *(shop)* la pharmacie
**cheque** le chèque
**cheque book** le carnet de chèques
**cheque card** la carte bancaire
**cherry** la cerise
**chess** les échecs
**chest** la poitrine
**chewing gum** le chewing-gum
**chicken** le poulet
**child** l'enfant
**china** la porcelaine
**China** la Chine
**Chinese** chinois
**chips** les frites
**chocolate** le chocolat
 **box of chocolates** la boî te

de chocolats
**bar of chocolate** la tablette
de chocolat
**chop** *(food)* la côtelette
*(to cut)* hacher
**church** l'église
**cigar** le cigare
**cigarette** la cigarette
**cinema** le cinéma
**city** la ville
**city centre** le centre-ville
**class** la classe
**classical music** la musique
classique
**clean** propre
**clear** clair
**is that clear?** est-ce que c'est
clair?
**clever** intelligent
**clock** l'horloge
*(alarm)* le réveil
**close** *(near)* près
*(stuffy)* étouffant
*(verb)* fermer
**the shop is closed** le magasin
est fermé
**clothes** les vêtements
**club** le club
*(cards)* trèfle
**clutch** l'embrayage
**coach** le car
*(of train)* la voiture
**coach station** la gare routière
**coat** le manteau
**coathanger** le cintre
**cockroach** le cafard
**coffee** le café
**coin** la pièce
**cold** *(illness)* le rhume
*(adj)* froid
**collar** le col
**collection** *(stamps etc)* la

collection
*(postal)* la levée
**colour** la couleur
**colour film** la pellicule couleur
**comb** *(noun)* le peigne
*(verb)* peigner
**come** venir
**I come from ...** je viens de ...
**we came last week** nous
sommes arrivés la semaine
dernière
**communication cord** la sonnette
d'alarme
**compact disc** le disque compact
**compartment** le compartiment
**complicated** compliqué
**concert** le concert
**conditioner** *(hair)* le baume après-
shampoing
**conductor** *(bus)* le receveur
*(orchestra)* le chef d'orchestre
**congratulations!** félicitations!
**constipation** la constipation
**consulate** le consulat
**contact lenses** les verres de
contact
**contraceptive** le contraceptif
**cook** *(noun)* le cuisinier
*(do cooking)* faire la cuisine
**cooking utensils** les ustensiles de
cuisine
**cool** frais
**cork** le bouchon
**corkscrew** le tire-bouchon
**corner** le coin
**corridor** le couloir
**Corsica** la Corse
**Corsican** corse
**cosmetics** les produits de beauté
**cost** *(verb)* coûter
**what does it cost?** combien ça
coûte?

107

**cotton** le coton
**cotton wool** le coton hydrophile
**cough** *(verb)* tousser
  *(noun)* la toux
**council** la municipalité
**country** *(state)* le pays
  *(not town)* la campagne
**cousin** *(male)* le cousin
  *(female)* la cousine
**crab** le crabe
**cramp** la crampe
**crayfish** *(freshwater)* l'écrevisse
  *(saltwater)* la langoustine
**cream** la crème
**credit card** la carte de crédit
**crew** l'équipage
**crisps** les chips
**crowded** bondé
**cruise** la croisière
**crutches** les béquilles
**cry** *(weep)* pleurer
  *(shout)* crier
**cucumber** le concombre
**cufflinks** les boutons de
  manchette
**cup** la tasse
**cupboard** le placard
**curlers** les rouleaux
**curls** les boucles
**curry** le curry
**curtain** le rideau
**cut** *(noun)* la coupure
  *(verb)* couper

**dad** papa
**dairy** *(shop)* la crémerie
**dark** foncé
**daughter** la fille
**day** le jour

**dead** mort
**deaf** sourd
**dear** cher
**deckchair** la chaise longue
**deep** profond
**deliberately** exprès
**dentist** le dentiste
**dentures** le dentier
**deny** nier
  **I deny it** je le nie
**deodorant** le déodorant
**department store** le grand
  magasin
**departure** le départ
**develop** *(grow)* se développer
  *(a film)* développer
**diamond** *(jewel)* le diamant
  *(cards)* carreau
**diarrhoea** la diarrhée
**diary** l'agenda
**dictionary** le dictionnaire
**die** mourir
**diesel** le diesel
**different** différent
  **that's different** c'est différent
  **I'd like a different one** j'en
voudrais un autre
**difficult** difficile
**dining car** le wagon-restaurant
**dining room** la salle à manger
**directory** le répertoire
  *(telephone)* l'annuaire
**dirty** sale
**disabled** handicapé
**distributor** *(car)* le delco
**dive** plonger
**diving board** le plongeoir
**divorced** divorcé
**do** faire
**doctor** le docteur
**document** le document
**dog** le chien

**doll** la poupée
**dollar** le dollar
**door** la porte
**double room** la chambre pour deux personnes
**doughnut** le beignet
**down** en bas
**drawing pin** la punaise
**dress** la robe
**drink** *(verb)* boire
    *(noun)* la boisson
    **would you like a drink?** voulez-vous boire quelque chose?
**drinking water** l'eau potable
**drive** *(verb: car)* conduire
**driver** le conducteur
**driving licence** le permis de conduire
**drunk** soûl
**dry** sec
**dry cleaner** le pressing
**during** pendant
**dustbin** la poubelle
**duster** le chiffon à poussière
**Dutch** hollandais
**duty-free** hors-taxe

**each** *(every)* chaque
    **two francs each** deux francs pièce
**early** tôt
**earrings** les boucles d'oreille
**ears** les oreilles
**east** l'est
**easy** facile
**egg** l'œuf
**egg cup** le coquetier
**either: either of them** n'importe lequel

**either ... or ...** soit ... soit ...
**elastic** élastique
**elastic band** l'élastique
**elbows** les coudes
**electric** électrique
**electricity** l'électricité
**else: something else** autre chose
    **someone else** quelqu'un d'autre
    **somewhere else** ailleurs
**embarrassing** gênant
**embassy** l'ambassade
**embroidery** la broderie
**emerald** l'émeraude
**emergency** l'urgence
**empty** vide
**end** la fin
**engaged** *(couple)* fiancé
    *(occupied)* occupé
**engine** *(motor)* le moteur
    *(railway)* la locomotive
**England** l'Angleterre
**English** anglais
**enlargement** l'agrandissement
**enough** assez
**entertainment** le divertissement
**entrance** l'entrée
**envelope** l'enveloppe
**escalator** l'escalier roulant
**especially** particulièrement
**evening** le soir
**every** chaque
**everyone** tout le monde
**everything** tout
**everywhere** partout
**example** l'exemple
    **for example** par exemple
**excellent** excellent
**excess baggage** l'excédent de bagages
**exchange** *(verb)* échanger
**exchange rate** le taux de change
**excursion** l'excursion

**excuse me!** pardon!
**exit** la sortie
**expensive** cher
**extension lead** la rallonge
**eye drops** les gouttes pour les
  yeux
**eyes** les yeux

**face** le visage
**faint** *(unclear)* vague
  *(verb)* s'évanouir
  **to feel faint** se trouver mal
**fair** *(funfair)* la foire
  *(just)* juste
  **it's not fair** ce n'est pas juste
**false teeth** le dentier
**fan** *(ventilator)* le ventilateur
  *(enthusiast)* le fan
**fan belt** la courroie du ventilateur
**far** loin
**fare** le prix du billet
**farm** la ferme
**farmer** le fermier
**fashion** la mode
**fast** rapide
**fat** *(of person)* gros
  *(on meat etc)* la graisse
**father** le père
**feel** *(touch)* toucher
  **I feel hot** j'ai chaud
  **I feel like ...** j'ai envie de ...
  **I don't feel well** je ne me sens
  pas bien
**feet** les pieds
**felt-tip pen** le feutre
**ferry** *(small)* le bac
  *(cross-Channel)* le ferry
**fever** la fièvre
**fiancé** le fiancé

**fiancée** la fiancée
**field** le champ
**fig** la figue
**filling** *(tooth)* le plombage
  *(sandwich etc)* la garniture
**film** le film
**finger** le doigt
**fire** le feu
  *(blaze)* l'incendie
**fire extinguisher** l'extincteur
**firework** le feu d'artifice
**first** premier
**first aid** les premiers soins
**first floor** le premier étage
**fish** le poisson
**fishing** la pêche
  **to go fishing** aller à la pêche
**fishing rod** la canne à pêche
**fishmonger** le poissonnier
**fizzy** pétillant
**flag** le drapeau
**flash** *(camera)* le flash
**flat** *(level)* plat
  *(apartment)* l'appartement
**flavour** le goût
**flight** le vol
**flip-flops** les tongs
**flippers** les palmes
**flour** la farine
**flower** la fleur
**flu** la grippe
**flute** la flûte
**fly** *(verb)* voler
  *(insect)* la mouche
**fog** le brouillard
**folk music** la musique folklorique
**food** la nourriture
**food poisoning** l'intoxication
  alimentaire
**foot** le pied
**football** le football
**for** pour

**for me** pour moi
**what for?** pour quoi faire?
**for a week** pour une semaine
**foreigner** l'étranger
**forest** la forêt
**fork** la fourchette
**fortnight** quinze jours
**fountain pen** le stylo-plume
**fracture** la fracture
**France** la France
**free** *(no cost)* gratuit
*(at liberty)* libre
**freezer** le congélateur
**French** français
**fridge** le frigo
**friend** l'ami
**friendly** amical
**front: in front** devant
**frost** la gelée
**fruit** le fruit
**fruit juice** le jus de fruit
**fry** frire
**frying pan** la poêle à frire
**full** complet
**I'm full** j'ai l'estomac bien
rempli!
**full board** la pension complète
**funnel** *(for pouring)* l'entonnoir
**funny** drôle
**furniture** les meubles

**garage** le garage
**garden** le jardin
**garlic** l'ail
**gas-permeable lenses** les lentilles
semi-rigides
**gay** *(happy)* gai
*(homosexual)* homosexuel
**gear** la vitesse

**gear lever** le levier de vitesse
**gents** *(toilet)* les toilettes
**German** allemand
**Germany** l'Allemagne
**get** *(fetch)* aller chercher
**have you got ...?** avez-vous ...?
**to get the train** prendre le train
**get back: we get back
tomorrow** nous rentrons demain
**to get something back**
récupérer quelque chose
**get in** entrer
*(arrive)* arriver
**get out** sortir
**get up** *(rise)* se lever
**gift** le cadeau
**gin** le gin
**ginger** le gingembre
**girl** la fille
**girlfriend** la petite amie
**give** donner
**glad** heureux
**I'm glad** je suis ravi
**glass** le verre
**glasses** les lunettes
**gloss prints** les épreuves sur
papier glacé
**gloves** les gants
**glue** la colle
**goggles** les lunettes de plongée
**gold** l'or
**good** *(adj)* bon
**good!** bien!
**goodbye** au revoir
**government** le gouvernement
**grapes** le raisin
**grass** l'herbe
**green** vert
**grey** gris
**grill** le gril
**grocer** *(shop)* l'épicerie
**ground floor** le rez-de-chaussée

**ground sheet** le tapis de sol
**guarantee** *(noun)* la garantie
  *(verb)* garantir
**guard** le garde
  *(train)* le chef de train
**guide book** le guide
**guitar** la guitare
**gun** *(rifle)* le fusil
  *(pistol)* le pistolet

**hair** les cheveux
**haircut** la coupe (de cheveux)
**hairdresser** le coiffeur
**hair dryer** le sèche-cheveux
**hair spray** la laque
**half** demi
  **half an hour** la demi-heure
**half board** la demi-pension
**ham** le jambon
**hamburger** le hamburger
**hammer** le marteau
**hand** la main
**hand brake** le frein à main
**handbag** le sac à main
**handkerchief** le mouchoir
**handle** *(door)* la poignée
**handsome** beau
**hangover** la gueule de bois
**happy** heureux
**harbour** le port
**hard** dur
**hard lenses** les lentilles rigides
**hat** le chapeau
**have** avoir
  **can I have ...?** puis-je avoir ...?
  **have you got ...?** avez-vous ...?
  **I have to go now** il faut que
  parte
**hayfever** le rhume des foins

**he** il
**head** la tête
**headache** le mal de tête
**headlights** les phares
**hear** entendre
**hearing aid** l'appareil acoustique
**heart** *(also cards)* le cœur
**heart attack** la crise cardiaque
**heating** le chauffage
**heavy** lourd
**heel** le talon
**hello** bonjour
  *(to get attention)* hé!
**help** *(noun)* l'aide
  *(verb)* aider
  **help!** au secours!
**her: it's her** c'est elle
  **it's for her** c'est pour elle
  **give it to her** donne-le-lui
  **her book** son livre
  **her house** sa maison
  **her shoes** ses chaussures
  **it's hers** c'est à elle
**here** ici
**hi** salut
**high** haut
**highway code** le code de la route
**hill** la colline
**him: it's him** c'est lui
  **it's for him** c'est pour lui
  **give it to him** donne-le-lui
**his: his book** son livre
  **his house** sa maison
  **his shoes** ses chaussures
  **it's his** c'est à lui
**history** l'histoire
**hitch hike** faire du stop
**hobby** le passe-temps
**Holland** la Hollande
**holiday** les vacances
**honest** honnête
**honey** le miel

**honeymoon** la lune de miel
**horn** *(car)* le klaxon
  *(animal)* la corne
**horrible** horrible
**hospital** l'hôpital
**hot** chaud
**hot water bottle** la bouillotte
**hour** l'heure
**house** la maison
**how?** comment?
**hungry: to be hungry** avoir faim
  **I'm hungry** j'ai faim
**husband** le mari

**I** je
**ice** la glace
**ice cream** la glace
**ice cube** le glaçon
**ice lolly** l'esquimau
**ice rink** la patinoire
**ice-skates** les patins à glace
**if** si
**ignition** l'allumage
**immediately** immédiatement
**impossible** impossible
**in** dans
  **in France** en France
**India** l'Inde
**Indian** indien
**indicator** le clignotant
**indigestion** l'indigestion
**infection** l'infection
**information** l'information
**injection** la piqûre
**injury** la blessure
**ink** l'encre
**inn** l'auberge
**inner tube** la chambre à air
**insect** l'insecte

**insect repellent** la crème
  anti-insecte
**insomnia** l'insomnie
**insurance** l'assurance
**interesting** intéressant
**invitation** l'invitation
**Ireland** l'Irlande
**Irish** irlandais
**iron** *(metal)* le fer
  *(for clothes)* le fer à repasser
**ironmonger** la quincaillerie
**is: he/she is** il/elle est
  **it is** c'est
**island** l'île
**it** il, elle
**Italian** italien
**Italy** l'Italie
**itch** *(noun)* la démangeaison
  *(verb)* démanger
  **it itches** ça me démange
**its** son, sa, ses *(see his)*

**jacket** la veste
**jacuzzi** le jacousi
**jam** la confiture
**jazz** le jazz
**jealous** jaloux
**jeans** les jeans
**jellyfish** la méduse
**jeweller** le bijoutier
**job** le travail
**jog** *(verb)* faire du jogging
  **to go for a jog** aller faire du
  jogging
**joke** la plaisanterie
**journey** le voyage
**jumper** le pull
**just: it's just arrived** ça vient
  juste d'arriver

**I've just one left** il n'en reste plus qu'un

**kettle** la bouilloire
**key** la clé
**kidney** le rein
  *(food)* les rognons
**kilo** le kilo
**kilometre** le kilomètre
**kitchen** la cuisine
**knee** le genou
**knife** le couteau
**knit** tricoter
**knitting needle** l'aiguille à tricoter

**label** l'étiquette
**lace** la dentelle
  *(of shoe)* le lacet
**ladies** *(toilet)* les toilettes
**lake** le lac
**lamb** l'agneau
**lamp** la lampe
**lampshade** l'abat-jour
**land** *(noun)* la terre
  *(verb)* atterrir
**language** la langue
**large** grand
**last** *(final)* dernier
  **last week** la semaine dernière
  **last month** le mois dernier
  **at last!** enfin!
**late: it's getting late** il se fait tard
  **the bus is late** le bus est en retard

**laugh** rire
**launderette** le lavomatic
**laundry** *(place)* la blanchisserie
  *(clothes)* le linge
**laxative** le laxatif
**lazy** fainéant
**leaf** la feuille
**learn** apprendre
**leather** le cuir
**left** *(not right)* la gauche
  **there is nothing left** il ne reste plus rien
**left luggage** la consigne
  *(locker)* la consigne automatique
**leftovers** les restes
**leg** la jambe
**lemon** le citron
**lemonade** la limonade
**length** la longueur
**lens** *(camera)* l'objectif
**less** moins
**lesson** la leçon
**letter** la lettre
**letterbox** la boîte aux lettres
**lettuce** la laitue
**library** la bibliothèque
**licence** le permis
**life** la vie
**lift** *(in building)* l'ascenceur
  **to give someone a lift** reconduire quelqu'un
**light** *(not heavy)* léger
  *(not dark)* clair
**light meter** la cellule photoélectrique
**lighter** le briquet
**lighter fuel** le gaz à briquet
**like: I like you** je vous aime bien
  **I like swimming** j'aime nager
  **it's like ...** c'est comme ...
**lime** *(fruit)* le citron vert
**lip salve** le baume pour les lèvres

**lipstick** le rouge à lèvres
**liqueur** la liqueur
**list** la liste
**litre** le litre
**litter** les ordures
**little** *(small)* petit
  **it's a little big** c'est un peu
  trop grand
**liver** le foie
**lobster** le homard
**lollipop** la sucette
**lorry** le camion
**lost property** les objets trouvés
**lot: a lot** beaucoup
**loud** fort
  *(colour)* criard
**lounge** le salon
**love** *(noun)* l'amour
  *(verb)* aimer
**lover** l'amant
**low** bas
**luck** la chance
  **good luck!** bonne chance!
**luggage** les bagages
**luggage rack** le porte-bagages
**lunch** le déjeuner
**Luxembourg** le Luxembourg

**magazine** la revue
**mail** le courrier
**make** faire
**manager** le directeur
**map** la carte
  *(street map)* le plan
**margarine** la margarine
**market** le marché
**marmalade** la confiture d'oranges
**married** marié
**mascara** le mascara

**mass** *(church)* la messe
**match** *(light)* l'allumette
  *(sport)* le match
**material** *(cloth)* le tissu
**mattress** le matelas
**maybe** peut-être
**me: it's me** c'est moi
  **it's for me** c'est pour moi
  **give it to me** donne-le-moi
**meal** le repas
**meat** la viande
**mechanic** le mécanicien
**medicine** le médicament
**Mediterranean** la Méditerranée
**meeting** la réunion
**melon** le melon
**menu** le menu
**message** le message
**midday** midi
**middle** le milieu
**midnight** minuit
**milk** le lait
**mine: it's mine** c'est à moi
**mineral water** l'eau minérale
**mirror** le miroir
  *(car)* le rétroviseur
**mistake** l'erreur
  **to make a mistake** se tromper
**money** l'argent
**month** le mois
**monument** le monument
**moped** la mobylette (R)
**more** plus
  **more or less** plus ou moins
**morning** le matin
  **in the morning** dans la
  matinée
**Moroccan** marocain
**Morocco** le Maroc
**mother** la mère
**motorbike** la moto
**motorboat** le bateau à moteur

**motorway** l'autoroute
**mountain** la montagne
**moustache** la moustache
**mouth** la bouche
**move** bouger
  **don't move!** ne bougez pas!
  *(house)* déménager
**much: not much** pas beaucoup
**mug** la tasse
  **a mug of coffee** un bol de café
**mum** maman
**museum** le musée
**mushroom** le champignon
**music** la musique
**musical instrument** l'instrument
de musique
**musician** le musicien
**mussels** les moules
**mustard** la moutarde
**my: my book** mon livre
  **my house** ma maison
  **my shoes** mes chaussures

**nail** *(metal)* le clou
  *(finger)* l'ongle
**nail file** la lime à ongles
**nail polish** le vernis à ongles
**narrow** étroit
**near: near the door** près de la
porte
  **near London** près de Londres
**neck** le cou
**necklace** le collier
**need** *(verb)* avoir besoin de
  **I need ...** j'ai besoin de ...
  **there's no need** ce n'est pas
nécessaire
**needle** l'aiguille
**negative** *(photo)* le négatif

  *(no)* négatif
**neither: neither of them** ni l'un
ni l'autre
  **neither ... nor ...** ni ... ni ...
**nephew** le neveu
**never** jamais
**new** nouveau
**news** les nouvelles
  *(TV)* les informations
**newsagent** le tabac-journaux
**newspaper** le journal
**New Zealand** la Nouvelle
Zélande
**next** prochain
  **next week** la semaine prochaine
  **next month** le mois prochain
  **what next?** et puis quoi encore?
**niece** la nièce
**night** la nuit
**nightclub** la boîte de nuit
**nightdress** la chemise de nuit
**no** *(response)* non
  *(not any)* aucun
**noisy** bruyant
**north** le nord
**nose** le nez
**nose drops** les gouttes pour le
nez
**not** pas
**notebook** le carnet
**novel** le roman
**now** maintenant
**nudist** le nudiste
**number** le nombre
  *(telephone)* le numéro
**number plate** la plaque
d'immatriculation
**nurse** l'infirmière
**nursery slope** la pente pour
débutants
**nut** *(fruit)* la noix
  *(for bolt)* l'écrou

occasionally de temps en temps
office le bureau
often souvent
oil l'huile
ointment la pommade
old vieux
olive l'olive
omelette l'omelette
on sur
onion l'oignon
open *(verb)* ouvrir
  *(adj)* ouvert
operator *(phone)* l'opératrice
opposite en face
optician l'opticien
or ou
orange *(colour)* orange
  *(fruit)* l'orange
orchestra l'orchestre
organ l'organe
  *(music)* l'orgue
our notre, nos
  it's ours c'est à nous
out: he's out il n'est pas là
outside dehors
over par-dessus
  over there là-bas
overtake doubler
oyster l'huître

pack of cards le jeu de cartes
package le paquet
  *(parcel)* le colis
packet le paquet
  a packet of ... un paquet de ...

page la page
pain la douleur
pair la paire
Pakistan le Pakistan
Pakistani pakistanais
pancake la crêpe
paracetamol le comprimé de
  paracétamol
paraffin le pétrole
parcel le colis
pardon? pardon?
parents les parents
park *(noun)* le jardin public
  *(verb)* garer
parsley le persil
party *(celebration)* une fête
  *(group)* le groupe
  *(political)* le parti
passenger le passager
passport le passeport
pasta les pâtes
path le chemin
pay payer
peach la pêche
peanuts les cacahuètes
pear la poire
pearl la perle
peas les petits pois
pedestrian le piéton
peg *(clothes)* la pince à linge
pen le stylo
pencil le crayon
pencil sharpener le taille-crayon
penfriend le correspondant
penknife le canif
pepper *(& salt)* le poivre
  *(red/green)* le poivron
peppermints les bonbons à la
  menthe
perfume le parfum
perhaps peut-être
perm la permanente

117

**petrol** l'essence
**petrol station** la station-service
**petticoat** le jupon
**photograph** *(noun)* la photo
*(verb)* photographier
**photographer** le photographe
**phrase book** le recueil
d'expressions
**piano** le piano
**pickpocket** le pickpocket
**picnic** le pique-nique
**piece** le morceau
**pillow** l'oreiller
**pilot** le pilote
**pin** l'épingle
**pineapple** l'ananas
**pink** rose
**pipe** *(for smoking)* la pipe
*(for water)* le tuyau
**piston** le piston
**piston ring** le segment de piston
**pizza** la pizza
**plant** la plante
**plaster** *(for cut)* le pansement
**plastic** le plastique
**plastic bag** le sac en plastique
**plate** l'assiette
**platform** le quai
**please** s'il vous plaît
**plug** *(electrical)* la prise
*(sink)* le bouchon
**pocket** la poche
**poison** le poison
**policeman** l'agent de police
**police station** le commissariat
**politics** la politique
**poor** pauvre
*(bad quality)* mauvais
**pop music** la musique pop
**pork** le porc
**port** *(harbour)* le port
*(drink)* le porto

**porter** le porteur
**Portugal** le Portugal
**Portuguese** portugais
**post** *(noun)* la poste
*(verb)* poster
**post box** la boîte aux lettres
**postcard** la carte postale
**poster** l'affiche
**postman** le facteur
**post office** la poste
**potato** la pomme de terre
**poultry** la volaille
**pound** *(money, weight)* la livre
**powder** la poudre
**pram** le landau
**prawn** la crevette
**prescription** l'ordonnance
**pretty** *(beautiful)* joli
*(quite)* plutôt
**priest** le prêtre
**private** privé
**problem** le problème
**what's the problem?** qu'est-ce
qui ne va pas?
**public** le public
**pull** tirer
**purple** violet
**purse** le porte-monnaie
**push** pousser
**pushchair** la poussette
**pyjamas** le pyjama
**Pyrenees** les Pyrénées

**quality** la qualité
**quay** le quai
**question** la question
**queue** *(noun)* la queue
*(verb)* faire la queue
**quick** rapide

**quiet** silencieux
**quilt** la couette
**quite** *(fairly)* assez
  *(fully)* très

**radiator** le radiateur
**radio** la radio
**radish** le radis
**railway line** la ligne de chemin
  de fer
  *(track)* la voie ferrée
**rain** la pluie
**raincoat** l'imperméable
**raisin** le raisin sec
**rare** *(uncommon)* rare
  *(steak)* bleu
**raspberry** la framboise
**razor blades** les lames de
  rasoir
**reading lamp** la lampe de
  bureau
  *(bed)* la lampe de chevet
**ready** prêt
**rear lights** les feux arrière
**receipt** le reçu
**receptionist** la réceptionniste
**record** *(music)* le disque
  *(sporting etc)* le record
**record player** le tourne-disque
**record shop** le disquaire
**red** rouge
**refreshments** les rafraîchissements
**registered letter** la lettre
  recommandée
**relax** se détendre
**religion** la religion
**remember** se rappeler
**reservation** la réservation
**rest** *(remainder)* le reste

  *(relax)* se reposer
**restaurant** le restaurant
**restaurant car** la voiture de
  restauration
**return** *(come back)* revenir
  *(give back)* rendre
**rice** le riz
**rich** riche
**right** *(correct)* juste
  *(direction)* la droite
**ring** *(to call)* appeler
  *(wedding etc)* la bague
**ripe** mûr
**river** la rivière
  *(big)* le fleuve
**road** la route
**rock** *(stone)* le rocher
  *(music)* le rock
**roll** *(bread)* le petit pain
  *(verb)* rouler
**roller skates** les patins à
  roulettes
**room** la chambre
  *(space)* la place
**rope** la corde
**rose** la rose
**round** *(circular)* rond
  **it's my round** c'est ma
  tournée
**rowing boat** la barque
**rubber** *(eraser)* la gomme
  *(material)* le caoutchouc
**rubbish** les ordures
**ruby** *(colour)* rubis
  *(stone)* le rubis
**rucksack** le sac à dos
**rug** *(mat)* la carpette
  *(blanket)* la couverture
**ruins** les ruines
**ruler** la règle
**rum** le rhum
**runway** la piste

sad triste

safe en sécurité

safety pin l'épingle de nourrice

sailing boat le voilier

salad la salade

salami le salami

sale la vente
*(at reduced prices)* les soldes

salmon le saumon

salt le sel

same: the same hat le même chapeau
the same dress la même robe

sand le sable

sandals les sandales

sand dunes les dunes

sandwich le sandwich

sanitary towels les serviettes périodiques

sauce la sauce

saucepan la poêle

sauna le sauna

sausage la saucisse

say dire
what did you say? qu'avez-vous dit?
how do you say...? comment dit-on ...?

scampi la langoustine

Scandinavia la Scandinavie

scarf l'écharpe

school l'école

scissors les ciseaux

Scotland l'Ecosse

Scottish écossais

screw la vis

screwdriver le tournevis

sea la mer

seat la place

seat belt la ceinture de sécurité

see voir
I can't see je ne vois rien
I see je vois

sell vendre

sellotape (R) le scotch (R)

serious sérieux

serviette la serviette

several plusieurs

sew coudre

shampoo le shampoing

shave *(noun)* le rasage
*(verb)* se raser

shaving foam la mousse à raser

shawl le châle

she elle

sheet le drap

shell la coquille

sherry le sherry

ship le bateau

shirt la chemise

shoe laces les lacets

shoe polish le cirage

shoe shop le magasin de chaussures

shoes les chaussures

shop le magasin

shopping les courses
to go shopping faire des courses

shopping centre le centre commercial

short court

shorts le short

shoulder l'épaule

shower *(bath)* la douche
*(rain)* l'averse

shrimp la crevette

shutter *(camera)* l'obturateur
*(window)* le volet

sick *(ill)* malade
I feel sick j'ai envie de vomir

**side** le côté
  *(edge)* le bord
  **I'm on her side** je suis
  d'accord avec elle
**sidelights** les veilleuses
**silk** la soie
**silver** *(colour)* argenté
  *(metal)* l'argent
**simple** simple
**sing** chanter
**single** *(one)* seul
  *(unmarried)* célibataire
**single room** la chambre pour une
  personne
**sister** la sœur
**skates** les patins à glace
**ski** *(noun)* le ski
  *(verb)* skier
  **to go skiing** faire du ski
**skid** *(verb)* déraper
**ski lift** le remonte-pente
**skin cleanser** le lait démaquillant
**skirt** la jupe
**ski stick** le bâton de ski
**sky** le ciel
**sledge** la luge
**sleep** *(noun)* le sommeil
  *(verb)* dormir
  **to go to sleep** s'endormir
**sleeping bag** le sac de couchage
**sleeping car** le wagon-lit
**sleeping pill** le somnifère
**sling** l'écharpe
**slippers** les pantoufles
**slow** lent
**small** petit
**smell** *(noun)* l'odeur
  *(verb)* sentir
**smile** *(noun)* le sourire
  *(verb)* sourire
**smoke** *(noun)* la fumée
  *(verb)* fumer

**snack** le snack
**snorkel** le tuba
**snow** la neige
**so** si
**soaking solution** *(for contact
  lenses)* la solution de trempage
**soap** le savon
**socks** les chaussettes
**soda water** l'eau gazeuse
**soft lenses** les lentilles souples
**somebody** quelqu'un
**somehow** d'une façon ou d'une
  autre
**something** quelque chose
**sometimes** quelquefois
**somewhere** quelque part
**son** le fils
**song** la chanson
**sorry!** pardon!
  **I'm sorry** je suis désolé
**soup** la soupe
**south** le sud
**South Africa** l'Afrique du Sud
**South African** sud-africain
**souvenir** le souvenir
**spade** *(shovel)* la pelle
  *(cards)* pique
**Spain** l'Espagne
**Spanish** espagnol
**spanner** la clé
**spares** les pièces de rechange
**spark(ing) plug** la bougie
**speak** parler
  **do you speak...?** parlez-vous...?
  **I don't speak...** je ne parle
  pas...
**speed** la vitesse
**speed limit** la limitation de
  vitesse
**speedometer** le compteur de
  vitesse
**spider** l'araignée

**spinach** les épinards
**spoon** la cuillère
**sprain** l'entorse
**spring** *(mechanical)* le ressort
   *(season)* le printemps
**stadium** le stade
**staircase** l'escalier
**stairs** les escaliers
**stamp** le timbre
**stapler** l'agrafeuse
**star** l'étoile
   *(film)* la vedette
**start** le départ
   *(verb)* commencer
**station** la gare
   *(tube)* la station
**statue** la statue
**steak** le steak
**steamer** le bateau à vapeur
   *(cooking)* le couscoussier
**steering wheel** le volant
**steward** le steward
**sting** *(noun)* la piqûre
   *(verb)* piquer
   **it stings** ça pique
**stockings** les bas
**stomach** l'estomac
**stomach-ache** le mal au ventre
**stop** *(verb)* s'arrêter
   *(bus stop)* l'arrêt
   **stop!** stop!
**storm** la tempête
**strawberry** la fraise
**stream** le ruisseau
**string** *(cord)* la ficelle
   *(guitar etc)* la corde
**student** l'étudiant
**stupid** stupide
**suburbs** la banlieue
**sugar** le sucre
**suit** *(noun)* le costume
   *(verb)* convenir

   **it suits you** ça vous va bien
**suitcase** la valise
**sun** le soleil
**sunbathe** se faire bronzer
**sunburn** le coup de soleil
**sunglasses** les lunettes de soleil
**sunny** ensoleillé
**suntan** le bronzage
**suntan lotion** le lait solaire
**supermarket** le supermarché
**supplement** le supplément
**sweat** *(noun)* la transpiration
   *(verb)* transpirer
**sweatshirt** le sweat-shirt
**sweet** *(not sour)* sucré
   *(candy)* le bonbon
**swimming costume** le maillot de bain
**swimming pool** la piscine
**swimming trunks** le maillot de bain
**Swiss** suisse
**switch** l'interrupteur
**Switzerland** la Suisse
**synagogue** la synagogue

**table** la table
**tablet** un comprimé
**take** prendre
**take off** *(plane) (noun)* le décollage
   *(verb)* décoller
**take-away** à emporter
**talcum powder** le talc
**talk** *(noun)* la conversation
   *(verb)* parler
**tall** grand
**tampon** le tampon
**tangerine** la mandarine
**tap** le robinet

**tapestry** la tapisserie
**tea** le thé
**tea towel** le torchon
**telegram** le télégramme
**telephone** *(noun)* le téléphone
  *(verb)* téléphoner
**telephone box** la cabine
  téléphonique
**telephone call** le coup de
  téléphone
**television** la télévision
**temperature** la température
**tent** la tente
**tent peg** le piquet de tente
**tent pole** le montant de tente
**than** que
**thank** *(verb)* remercier
  **thanks** merci
  **thank you** merci
**that: that bus** ce bus
  **that man** cet homme
  **that woman** cette femme
  **what's that?** qu'est-ce que c'est?
  **I think that ...** je pense que ...
**their: their room** leur chambre
  **their books** leurs livres
  **it's theirs** c'est à eux
**them: it's them** ce sont eux/elles
  **it's for them** c'est pour eux/elles
  **give it to them** donne-le-leur
**then** alors
**there** là
**thermos flask** la thermos
**these: these things** ces choses
  **these are mine** ils sont à moi
**they** ils/elles
**thick** épais
**thin** mince
**think** penser
  **I think so** je pense que oui
  **I'll think about it** je vais y
  penser

**thirsty: I'm thirsty** j'ai soif
**this: this bus** ce bus
  **this man** cet homme
  **this woman** cette femme
  **what's this?** qu'est-ce que c'est?
  **this is Mr ...** je vous présente
  M. ...
**those: those things** ces choses-là
  **those are his** ils sont à lui
**throat** la gorge
**throat pastilles** les pastilles pour
  la gorge
**through** à travers
**thunderstorm** l'orage
**ticket** le billet
  *(tube, bus)* le ticket
**tide** la marée
**tie** *(noun)* la cravate
  *(verb)* nouer
**tights** les collants
**time** l'heure
  **what's the time?** quelle heure
  est-il?
**timetable** l'horaire
**tin** la boîte de conserve
**tin opener** l'ouvre-boîte
**tip** *(money)* le pourboire
  *(end)* le bout
**tired** fatigué
  **I feel tired** je suis fatigué
**tissues** les kleenex (R)
**to: to England** en Angleterre
  **to the station** à la gare
  **to the doctor** chez le docteur
**toast** le pain grillé
**tobacco** le tabac
**toboggan** le toboggan
**today** aujourd'hui
**together** ensemble
**toilet** les toilettes
**toilet paper** le papier hygiénique
**tomato** la tomate

**tomorrow** demain
**tongue** la langue
**tonic** un schweppes (R)
**tonight** ce soir
**too** *(also)* aussi
 *(excessive)* trop
**tooth** la dent
**toothache** le mal aux dents
**toothbrush** la brosse à dents
**toothpaste** le dentifrice
**torch** la lampe de poche
**tour** la visite
**tourist** le touriste
**towel** la serviette
**tower** la tour
**town** la ville
**town hall** l'hôtel de ville
**toy** le jouet
**toy shop** le magasin de jouets
**track suit** le survêtement
**tractor** le tracteur
**tradition** la tradition
**traffic** la circulation
**traffic lights** le feu
**trailer** la remorque
**train** le train
**translate** traduire
**transmission** la transmission
**travel agency** l'agence de
 voyage
**traveller's cheque** le chèque de
 voyage
**tray** le plateau
**tree** l'arbre
**trousers** le pantalon
**try** essayer
**Tunisia** la Tunisie
**Tunisian** tunisien
**tunnel** le tunnel
**tweezers** la pince à épiler
**typewriter** la machine à écrire
**tyre** le pneu

**umbrella** le parapluie
**uncle** l'oncle
**under** sous
**underground** le métro
**underpants** le slip
**university** l'université
**unmarried** célibataire
**until** jusqu'à
**unusual** inhabituel
**up** en haut
 *(upwards)* vers le haut
**urgent** urgent
**us: it's us** c'est nous
 **it's for us** c'est pour nous
 **give it to us** donnez-le-nous
**use** *(verb)* utiliser
 **it's no use** ça ne sert à rien
**useful** utile
**usual** habituel
**usually** d'habitude

**vacancy** *(room)* chambre à louer
**vacuum cleaner** l'aspirateur
**vacuum flask** la thermos
**valley** la vallée
**valve** la soupape
**vanilla** la vanille
**vase** le vase
**veal** le veau
**vegetables** les légumes
**vegetarian** *(person)* le végétarien
 *(adj)* végétarien
**vehicle** le véhicule
**very** très
**vest** le tricot de corps

**view** la vue
**viewfinder** le viseur
**villa** la villa
**village** le village
**vinegar** le vinaigre
**violin** le violon
**visa** le visa
**visit** *(noun)* la visite
  *(verb)* visiter
**visitor** le visiteur
**vitamin tablet** le comprimé de
  vitamines
**vodka** la vodka
**voice** la voix

**wait** attendre
**waiter** le serveur
  **waiter!** garçon, s'il vous plaît!
**waiting room** la salle d'attente
**waitress** la serveuse
**Wales** le pays de Galles
**walk** *(verb)* marcher
  **to go for a walk** aller se
  promener
**walkman (R)** le walkman (R)
**wall** *(inside)* la paroi
  *(outside)* le mur
**wallet** le portefeuille
**war** la guerre
**wardrobe** l'armoire
**warm** chaud
**was: I was** j'étais
  **he was** il était
  **she was** elle était
  **it was** il/elle était
**washing powder** la lessive
**washing-up liquid** le produit
  pour la vaisselle
**wasp** la guêpe

**watch** *(noun)* la montre
  *(verb)* regarder
**water** l'eau
**waterfall** la chute d'eau
**wave** *(noun)* la vague
  *(verb)* faire signe de la main
**we** nous
**weather** le temps
**wedding** le mariage
**week** la semaine
**wellingtons** les bottes en
  caoutchouc
**Welsh** gallois
**were: you were** vous étiez
  *(singular familiar)* tu étais
  **we were** nous étions
  **they were** ils/elles étaient
**west** l'ouest
**wet** mouillé
**what?** comment?
  **what is it?** qu'est-ce que c'est?
**wheel** la roue
**wheelchair** le fauteuil roulant
**when?** quand?
**where?** où?
**whether** si
**which?** lequel?
**whisky** le whisky
**white** blanc
**who?** qui?
**why?** pourquoi?
**wide** large
**wife** l'épouse
**wind** le vent
**window** la fenêtre
**windscreen** le pare-brise
**windscreen wiper** l'essuie-glace
**wine** le vin
**wine list** la carte des vins
**wine merchant** le négociant en
  vins
**wing** l'aile

**with** avec
**without** sans
**wood** le bois
**wool** la laine
**word** le mot
**work** *(noun)* le travail
  *(verb)* travailler
  *(machine etc)* fonctionner
**worse** pire
**wrapping paper** le papier
  d'emballage
  *(for presents)* le papier cadeau
**wrist** le poignet
**writing paper** le papier à lettres
**wrong** faux

**yet** déjà
  **is it ready yet?** est-ce que c'est
  prêt?
  **not yet** pas encore
**yoghurt** le yaourt
**you** vous
  *(singular familiar)* tu
**your** *(singular familiar)*
  **your book** ton livre
  **your house** ta maison
  **your shoes** tes chaussures
  **it's yours** c'est à toi
  *(singular polite, plural)*
  **your house** votre maison
  **your shoes** vos chaussures
  **it's yours** c'est à vous
**youth hostel** l'auberge de jeunesse

**year** l'année
**yellow** jaune
**yes** oui
**yesterday** hier

**zip** la fermeture éclair (R)
**zoo** le zoo